LEON

FAST & FREE

FREE-FROM RECIPES FOR PEOPLE WHO REALLY LIKE FOOD

BY JANE BAXTER & JOHN VINCENT

conran
OCTOPUS

CONTENTS

LEON.
FAST & FREE

**THIS BOOK IS A BOOK FOR PEOPLE WHO WANT TO EAT WELL.
A FREE-FROM BOOK FOR PEOPLE WHO ACTUALLY LIKE FOOD.**

JOHN VINCENT

On one hand, this is the book that we should have written twelve years ago when we started LEON in 2004. It sums up why we began our adventure. We wanted to make it easy for everyone to eat well. On the other hand, the time for creating this book is now. Since we opened our first restaurant, our approach has gone from being radically alternative to almost mainstream.

From the start, we have believed in the power of food to delight, to invigorate, to bring people together. And we have believed too that the most healthy relationship with food is a positive and joyful one. But we also believe that modern industrialized food has made that relationship more opaque.

That is why at LEON, we look to make it easier for people to eat well and steer clear of things that they are either temporarily, or permanently, avoiding. Every recipe in this book is gluten-, dairy- and refined sugar-free. There are many other recipes which are nut-free, vegetarian, vegan, and even our version of paleo – Paleon.

You may be reading this because you have a serious medical condition and need to permanently steer clear of gluten, dairy, sugar, or something else entirely. You may be looking to cut out or reduce your exposure to these things because you are sensitive to them. There is also an increasing number of people who for now, or for keeps, are looking to 'eat clean' to avoid the ingredients that can cause inflammation, or issues with your stomach and gut. Then there are the rest. People who don't care at all about this stuff and just want some tasty, exciting dishes to make your life better. Well, you are welcome to this party too.

We have debated how much time to spend on the science bit. Not much, we concluded. The latest thinking on what we should cut back on, why, or when is available on your phone or laptop (as are alternative views from people who think the opposite). There are professional, well-trained and well-informed advisors who will help you get to the bottom of it, should you wish to. We've had lots of help along our free-from journey at LEON from nutritionists and food gurus and our job, we concluded, is to help you with the how – how to cook without these things whilst still enjoying your food very much.

The world doesn't need too many more cookbooks in general. What it does need, we believe, is a free-from book that doesn't compromise on flavour, foodiness or joy. A book that is naturally fast and naturally free. A book that leaves you free to love cooking, to enjoy eating and sharing your food with eagerness.

Within each section, there are broadly two types of dish: dishes that are naturally free-from (i.e. recipes we have developed that would not in any case need wheat, dairy or sugar), and dishes that typically rely on such ingredients (think: cake) that we have reimagined to avoid or replace these ingredients.

We hope that you like the result. If we have done our job right, we will have created a very safe, but very fun playground for you. Somewhere you can play without concern, and do so with a skip in your step. This book is intended to set you free.

All our recipes are created to be fast as well as free. Although some things may require patience, soaking overnight or resting to prove, there's no reason that eating freely should mean you can't have lots of stress-free free time. We begin with breakfast, and un-controversially move on to starters, everyday easy lunches and then speedy suppers. We have a dedicated section on sides and breads, and then go a bit more party-popper with starters and recipes for a crowd. Finally, to finish, it's all the tools you need to treat yourself. We wish you happy playing.

A WORD FROM JANE

As a professional cook who would quite happily dive face first into a vat of burrata or eat my body weight in grilled sourdough, I'm perhaps not the obvious choice to come up with a book of "free-from" recipes. To do that, the consensus seems to be that you have to be a glamorous ex model with thighs like a baby giraffe's and a penchant for courgetti, which, I hasten to add, I am not.

But this book is about the real world, not the airbrushed fantasy of glossy food magazines and advertising campaigns, and if there's one thing my 30-odd years in professional kitchens has taught me above all else, it's that the food you put on a plate has to taste fantastic if you're going win over an audience. That same philosophy is the guiding light for this, LEON's latest recipe collection. Many of the dishes you'll find in these

pages are influenced by my travels in southern Europe, south-east Asia and beyond, not least because there is an amazing number of food cultures out there in the wider world whose diet is naturally gluten- and dairy-free. Recipes such as Ethiopian flat bread using teff flour, fried tofu dumplings and Asian prawn pancakes are comforting, nourishing and will make your tastebuds sing. But while we have focused on those far-flung corners for inspiration, we have also adapted all kinds of time-honoured favourites from closer to home, to bring them into the "free from" fold. So there's no need to mourn your favourite sticky toffee pudding or eggs Florentine now that you're embracing a new way of eating.

I'm so happy to be able to share them with you all. Here's to freedom.

NUTRITIONAL KEY

Gluten-free, Dairy-free & Refined Sugar-free

Low Glycemic Load

Low Saturated Fat

Paleon

Nut-free

Vegetarian

Vegan

Contains Added Natural Unrefined Sugar*

No Added Sugar

* In some cases there may be unavoidable (but small) traces of refined sugar in bought ingredients, although nought has been added directly.

A WORD ON 'PALEON'

We think that the premise of the paleo diet is a great one. Eating natural, unprocessed food inspired by our cavemen ancestors. It makes a lot of sense. At LEON, we've interpreted our own version of Paleo – Paleon. Many agree on the main principles of paleo but there are disagreements on the margins of how it should be applied. For example, vinegar is a big grey area. It's more processed than is normally okay for the paleo diet, but if it contains no added sugar and is consumed in relatively sparing amounts where it is crucial to the recipe, then we give it a pass. Similarly, paleo preaches a low-sugar diet, but if you want to make a Paleo dessert for special occasions and the like, palm sugar is a good, low GL, natural, unrefined option. So again, we'll let it pass.

PALEON APROVED

FISH SAUCE

CURRY PASTE

SEA SALT

COCONUT AMINOS
a replacement for soy sauce

MUSTARD

STOCK

ARROWROOT POWDER

HERBS & SPICES

TAPIOCA FLOUR

UNSWEETENED COCOA

VANILLA

NATURAL SWEETENERS

MEAT

EGGS

FISH

FRUIT

SEEDS

VEGETABLES
sweet potatoes are okay

NUTS
not peanuts

QUINOA
another grey area that we approve

OILS & FATS
avocado, coconut, flaxseed, hazelnut, olive, ghee, sesame, walnut, macadamia, lard, tallow

WATER

HERBAL TEA

COFFEE

COCONUT WATER

FRESHLY JUICED FRUIT & VEG

CHIA SEEDS

NUTRITIONAL YEAST

PALEON NOT APROVED

PROCESSED FOODS

GRAINS:
wheat, corn, oats, rice, barley, millet, beer, spelt, rye, oats

LEGUMES:
all beans, chickpeas, lentils, peas, peanuts

SOY
edamame, tofu etc.

POTATOES

SUGAR
grey area as raw okay by some

DAIRY

VEGETABLE OILS
peanut, rapeseed, sunflower, corn, soybean, palm

ALCOHOL

SPICES

CAYENNE

ALLSPICE

CARAWAY

PINK PEPPERCORNS

CLOVES

FENUGREEK

NIGELLA SEEDS

SMOKED & SWEET PAPRIKA

BLACK & YELLOW
MUSTARD SEEDS

FENNEL SEEDS

CARDAMOM PODS

GROUND CINNAMON

CINNAMON STICKS

CUMIN

CORIANDER

NUTMEG

DRIED CHILLI FLAKES

TURMERIC

SAFFRON

CURRY POWDER

ASAFOETIDA

ONION POWDER

WILD OREGANO

POPPY SEEDS

STAR ANISE

SICHUAN PEPPERCORNS

FIVE-SPICE

GARAM MASALA

BAY LEAVES

SUMAC

ASIAN

FISH SAUCE

TAMARI

SAMBAL OELEK

COCONUT MILK
(from the coconut palm) is not actually nut-based and is brimming with health. Chock full of vitamins, minerals and good fats, it also delivers carbs, fibre and some protein. While it's a source of saturated fat, it's the good kind that's converted fast to energy and doesn't get stored as fat so readily.

CREAMED COCONUT
(in a block)

DESICCATED COCONUT

TAMARIND PASTE

RICE WINE

DRIED PRAWNS

CHILLI PASTE

MISO

WASABI PASTE

MIRIN

OILS & FATS

SESAME OIL

RICE BRAN OIL
comes from the outer layer of brown rice under the husk. Its high smoke point means it is well suited to high temperature cooking and baking. It's thought of as India's alternative to olive oil and contains some powerful antioxidants.

GRAPESEED OIL

OLIVE OIL
mild and extra virgin

PUMPKIN SEED OIL

SOYA SPREAD

COCONUT OIL

COCONUT BUTTER
includes the meat of the coconut as well as the oil, yielding a richer cooking texture. Health benefits include keeping you fuller for longer, supporting healthy weight management and packing an immune-boosting punch (from lauric acid).

HAZELNUT / WALNUT OIL

TRUFFLE OIL

PULSES
DRIED OR TINNED

YELLOW SPLIT PEAS

SPLIT MUNG BEANS

BORLOTTI

CANNELLINI

DAL

KIDNEY

CHICKPEAS

SPLIT FAVA

BLACK BEANS

PUY LENTILS

YOUR STORECUPBOARD

YOUR STORECUPBOARD

A well-stocked storecupboard is your ally in the fight for food freedom. We realize that some of these ingredients are harder to source than others, but remember this is just a steer in the right direction. You can find absolutely everything here online. Don't be intimidated; be creative and make substitutions and adjustments according to your tastes, your budget and of course, the size of your cupboard.

NUTS & SEEDS

PEANUTS

ALMONDS
flaked and white blanched (grind your own for freshness)

PUMPKIN, SUNFLOWER, SESAME SEEDS

PECANS

PINE NUTS

CASHEWS

HAZELNUTS

WALNUTS

MACADAMIA

PISTACHIOS

FLAX & CHIA SEEDS
are tiny powerhouses of health. They're a very good source of soluble fibre and are chock full of polyunsaturated fatty acids, antioxidants and protein. Chia seeds in particular are an excellent source of omega-3 fatty acids, which so many people are short on.

SWEET STUFF

DATE SYRUP

COCONUT SUGAR
(sometimes known as coconut palm sugar, or just palm sugar) is a natural sugar made from the sap of coconut trees. It retains many of the nutrients found in the coconut palm and is particularly rich in a complex of B vitamins, iron, potassium, magnesium and other essential minerals vital for maintaining good health. While it's still sugar, coconut sugar has a low GI (Glycaemic Index) of 35 (as opposed to glucose's 100) so is a better alternative to white table sugar. It also comes with it's own prebiotic fibre, inulin, which helps further slow down your body's response to the sweetness.

ERYTHRITOL
is a natural sweetener. It's called a sugar alcohol, but has no alcohol in it, and comes from the same family as xylitol. While not for everyone, e.g. people on low FODMAP diets, it gives a very natural, sweet taste to your baking and puds.

RAW HONEY
is one of nature's best friends – an alkaline-forming food that doesn't ferment in the stomach. Not only a natural source of sugar, but also of antioxidants, living enzymes and vitamins. Raw means it's unpasteurized, unheated and unprocessed, keeping all the living goodness intact.

MAPLE SYRUP
is made from the sweet sap of the Canadian maple tree and has been collected by indigenous peoples for hundreds of years. It's a source of minerals and antioxidants and, like raw honey and coconut sugar, is a healthier alternative to 'empty' white table sugar. The darker the colour, the better it is for baking.

RICE MALT SYRUP
(brown rice or syrup) is healthier than fructose (fruit sugar) or sucrose (white table sugar) because every cell in the body can use it immediately. Use sparingly though because it's still, although unrefined, a sugar.

YOUR STORE

CUPBOARD

RICE/GRAINS

SOBA NOODLES

BUCKWHEAT PASTA

BUCKWHEAT

QUINOA

POHA

RICE (Jasmine, glutinous, Arborio)

RICE NOODLES & WRAPPERS

BEAN CURD WRAPPERS

OTHER

COCONUT YOGHURT

is dairy-free, rich in the right kind of fats for healthy weight management, a good source of bone-building minerals and a vegan source of vitamin B12.

NON-DAIRY CREAMS

include soya and coconut creams. Your choice should be guided by taste, texture and function. Coconut cream for example can make a wonderful crème fraîche alternative, as well as a substitute for cream cheese icing on a carrot cake.

LARD

is an economical, neutral tasting, heat stable fat that is less vulnerable to becoming damaged (oxidized) during cooking. Contrary to common opinion, saturated fats like lard don't cause heart disease. Instead, they raise levels of good, protective cholesterol.

VEGETABLE SUET

is an alternative to meat-based suet and is low carb and low sodium. Check the labels of bought products, as some do contain gluten.

ALMOND MILK

is a tasty, nutrient-rich, dairy alternative for those without nut allergies or sensitivities. It works well for both sweet and savoury dishes, and can also be heated to make sauces.

DRIED APRICOTS

DATES

DRIED MANGO

DRIED FIGS

SULTANAS

RAISINS

VANILLA EXTRACT

SAUERKRAUT

PEANUT BUTTER

SEA SPAGHETTI

TORTILLA CHIPS

DAIRY-FREE MAYONNAISE

because you don't have to give up all your favourites just because you're dairy-free.

VINEGARS

including rice, coconut, white wine, cider, red wine, sherry, balsamic and muscatel

RED AND WHITE COOKING WINE

TINNED TOMATOES & PURÉE

DRIED PORCINI

MUSTARD

Dijon, wholegrain and powder

GLUTEN-FREE WORCESTERSHIRE SAUCE

TABASCO

GHERKINS

TAHINI

OLIVES

ANCHOVIES

PIQUILLO PEPPERS

CAPERS

BURMESE PICKLED TEA LEAVES

FLOURS & BAKING

GLUTEN-FREE PLAIN FLOUR

GLUTEN-FREE SELF RAISING FLOUR

GLUTEN-FREE BREAD FLOUR
that does not contain gums

RICE FLOUR (BROWN OR WHITE)

CORN-FLOUR

CORNMEAL

POLENTA

ALMOND FLOUR

TEFF FLOUR
comes from another ancient grain, about the size of a poppy seed, originating from around Ethiopia, where John has been about a dozen times. The flour has a mild nutty flavour and a healthy spread of amino acids, protein and iron. It's also a good source of resistant starch, a healthy fibre and calcium.

BUCKWHEAT
has nothing to do with wheat (it actually comes from the same family of plants as rhubarb). It's a gluten-free and robust flour that's great for baking bread, scones and pancakes.

GRAM FLOUR
comes from ground chickpeas. A staple in Asian countries, it's gluten-free and is perfect for things like pancakes and fritters.

COCONUT FLOUR
is high in fibre, healthy fats and protein. It lends a coarser, more fibrous texture to your baking. A highly digestible low glycaemic carb, it also has a slightly nutty flavour.

CHESTNUT FLOUR
is less well known than other gluten-free flours and can be pricey, but it's well worth it. Sweet, rich and intense, it's packed full of nutrition and was once an important food source for French and Italian peasants.

SORGHUM FLOUR
comes from another ancient grain that originated in Africa and Australia around 5,000 years ago. The kernel is ground into a slightly sweet, soft, fine flour which lends iron, B vitamins and protein to your baking.

QUINOA FLOUR
fits perfectly with our theme of using ancient, non-gluten containing grains to promote health. It's a versatile flour that gives a moist, fluffy crumb to your baking. Quinoa is a complete protein, meaning it contains all nine essential amino acids, plus iron, copper, vitamins and fibre.

MASA HARINA
is the dried flour made from masa (which in turn comes from corn), used in traditional Mexican cooking and to make tortillas and tamales. The method of making masa harina allows the protein and vitamins (like niacin and calcium) to be more easily absorbed when eaten. Don't mix it up with cornflour though which is made from a different process and has different qualities.

MILLET FLOUR
comes from an ancient grain that has been cultivated for over 10,000 years, with historic use in China and India predating the use of rice. It's very like wheat, but has no gluten so is a perfect alternative.

TAPIOCA STARCH
is used in gluten-free baking as an alternative to wheat flour. Extracted from the South American cassava plant, it has a slightly sweet flavour and improves the texture and 'chew' of baked goods, as well as helping to crisp crusts. It can also be used in place of cornflour for making sauces.

MODIFIED CASSAVA STARCH
(often known by its brand name, Baking Fix) is a bit of a hero when it comes to gluten-free cooking. A safe alternative to xanthan gum, it binds baked goods, emulsifies and thickens sauces, gravy and puds. It's sustainable and vegetable-based while bringing out the natural flavours in the food.

PSYLLIUM HUSKS AND POWDER
are a great, non-grain source of fibre which come from a species of herb called *Plantago ovata*. In gluten-free baking psyllium helps absorb moisture and make the texture less crumbly, while contributing all-important fibre – something that most people are really short on.

AGAR AGAR
is a gelling agent that comes from algae. Unlike gelatine, it's vegetarian and has no detectable scent or colour. It doesn't 'melt in the mouth' quite as quickly as gelatine, but can be used as a gelling agent for desserts, soups, ice cream and fruit preserves. We've also chosen it because it's high in minerals and hypo-allergenic for most.

ARROWROOT POWDER
is a mainstay of gluten-free cooking that helps to put the stretch and texture back into your foods. Derived from the roots of tropical plants. It has a long history of use for its healing properties. It will thicken your sauces, give your pastry and puds more texture.

DRIED YEAST

POTATO STARCH

GLUTEN-FREE OATS

BAKING POWDER

BICARBONATE OF SODA

CREAM OF TARTAR

WHY FREE-FROM?

From the inception of LEON we have labelled our dishes with icons that allow you to choose your food based on whether it is free from gluten or dairy, or on the extent to which it is likely to raise your blood sugar or adversely affect the good bacteria in your gut. Twelve years later, the interest in gluten, dairy and sugar has grown considerably. Both within nutritional science and in popular culture. Champion tennis players credit their success to eating free from gluten; TV presenters write books about how they feel having quit sugar; and most people have a friend who is ready to share their experience of eating 'clean'.

Beyond the anecdotal experiences and views of individuals is the scientific debate. We asked Meleni Aldridge, who specializes in reviewing the available science, to share her conclusions about what that science tells us. Not everyone will agree. And in fact for many people, even people with a suspicion that something is up, Meleni's conclusions may be quite controversial. Talk to us about it on Twitter, ask us questions, and take part in the debate.

Here are Meleni's conclusions. We hope they provide some new insights and some healthy food for thought.

MELENI ALDRIDGE BSc Nut Med, Dip cPNI

DAIRY, NOT THE STAPLE IT'S MADE OUT TO BE

Many people are increasingly turning away from dairy in search of alternatives that make them feel better, widen their diet and help reduce our livestock burden on the planet too. One of the most natural images in the world is that of a mother breastfeeding her baby and milk actually contains casomorphin, a feel-good component to ensure that babies keep coming back for more. This has a positive effect on the gut, calms the baby and helps the mother-baby bonding process.

Milk is the perfect food for babies because an infant's gut produces lactase, the enzyme needed to break down lactose (milk sugar). Unfortunately lactase production drastically reduces after weaning, making lactose intolerance the most common, and well studied, carbohydrate intolerance in the world. Lactose intolerance is the root of much distress and ill health among many and, while certain people might benefit from the right kind of dairy products, others can just increase their susceptibility to dairy-driven health problems. Numerous scientific studies (which we won't get into here) have linked dairy consumption to a wealth of problems including irritable bowel syndrome, obesity and autoimmune diseases. The body of literature is ever-growing and fascinating once you start reading it, but LEON are just here to help you enjoy a well-rounded, deliciously dairy-free diet, whatever your motives.

REFINED SUGAR – GETTING OFF THE WHITE ROLLERCOASTER

You'll struggle to find a person amongst us who hasn't experienced a 'sugar high', or its flip side, the 'sugar low'. Don't beat yourself up. Craving sugar is completely natural. Deep inside our genetic blueprint we're hardwired to seek out high calorie foods and consume as much of them as we can. Our very survival depended on it because these foods weren't readily available, so it didn't matter if we gorged on them a few times a year. Today it's a different matter. With our encoded desire for sweet, sugary foods, coupled with their availability on every street corner, you need a pretty strong will to turn in the opposite direction. Here are some sugar facts to help you make better choices.

Energy and water are the only essential requisites for life – and staying alive is a high energy business with every body system, organ and cell demanding to be kept replete so it can function optimally. Sugar, like all carbohydrates, converts to glucose, which is one of the key fuels our body uses. Our body will turn to glucose if fuel from healthy fats and protein isn't available. In the energy hierarchy, when it comes to allocating glucose, your brain is top dog, so each time you indulge in too many sugary, simple carb treats you'll get a huge sugar rush and then come crashing down. The desire to do it all over again then comes from your brain, which is starving because of a lack of energy-dense foods that fuel you for longer. Keeping this pattern going on a daily basis, year in and year out, puts us at much greater risk of type 2 diabetes, because our cells get more and more resistant to the insulin that the pancreas keeps pumping out in an effort to regulate blood sugar. Enter the white rollercoaster of blood sugar imbalance.

Remember though that carbs, specifically complex carbs (slow burning sugars), are critical for the body – not just for energy but also to construct cell membranes, for our connective tissues and for the metabolism of red blood cells. However, simple refined sugars (like sucrose and glucose) are fast fuels that are burned in minutes not hours. By not taking in sufficient protein, healthy fats and complex carbs, we simply keep our brain in permanent request and craving mode.

This entire book is free-from refined white table sugar. Instead, we've showcased a range of naturally-occurring sugars like coconut sugar, maple syrup, rice malt and raw honey, which come packed with other goodies from Nature's larder, including vitamins, minerals, antioxidants, trace elements and enzymes. We've then used combinations with protein and healthy fats to further slow their release into the body, help you to feel fuller and keep you from the turmoil of the white rollercoaster.

GLUTEN

All of a sudden the word gluten appears to be everywhere. The free-from aisle in the supermarket is dominated by gluten-free products and every third person you meet seems to want to avoid it.

SO WHAT IS GLUTEN?

Gluten is a family of proteins found in grains including wheat, rye and barley. If you ever made play dough as a child you'll remember the sticky, glutinous, pliable, heavy mound that was formed as soon as you added water to a bowl full of flour. That pliable solidity is due to the gluten in the wheat flour and this glutinous glue helps the foods made with these grains to hold their shape. But it can also wreak havoc in your gut – even if you don't feel a reaction.

FRIEND OR FOE?

Nature made our gut to behave best as a mostly sealed tube, with its own food factory (digestive processes), defence system (gut immune system), friends and partners (your gut bacteria) – a fully functioning microcosm with the purpose of generating energy and maintaining life. In return for a happy home, the right foods and social conditions, our gut bacteria and other microbes do their best to work tirelessly for us, digesting, creating compounds and co-factors, with the aim of protecting us throughout our lives. The whole shebang is policed and kept in balance by the gut's immune system. Problems start occurring when the happy balance is disturbed. Gluten can interfere with the zonulin, a peptide that controls regulators (known as the 'tight junctions') between the internal gut and the body

beyond. Zonulin is basically a gatekeeper, opening and closing the doors of the tight junctions to manage tiny molecules, both beneficial and harmful, within our gut and our bodies. When gluten interferes with the zonulin, the tube becomes 'leaky' with the tight junctions thrown wide open.

None of this escapes detection by your body's immune system. It gets busy mobilising a response – the strength and ferocity of which varies from individual to individual. Your immune system marks the gluten, as well as everything else floating out of your wide open tight junctions, as dangerous and creates a fire of inflammation to get rid of them. In some people the body's defence reaction to the leaked gut contents is swift and powerful, in others it takes longer before causing symptoms.

FREE AT LAST

The solution to bring order and balance to this chaos is simple. Allow the natural regulation of our tight junctions to be restored by removing the trigger in our diets that causes the disruption. Current estimates suggest that whilst only 1% of Western populations are formally diagnosed with coeliac disease, as many as 1 in 30 have a recognised sensitivity to gluten.

We're not saying gluten is the enemy, we're not telling you to steer clear from it entirely, we're offering you the option in this book to have completely gluten-free recipes, because we think they taste great that way.

1

GOOD MORNINGS

QUINOA FLORENTINE

Saturday morning magic. Go for a run first, and you will love yourself very much, and maybe a few other people too.

PREP TIME: 20 MINS · COOK TIME: 20 MINS

olive oil, for frying

100g **spinach**

2 tablespoons **olive oil**

150g **asparagus**, trimmed

4 **eggs**

salt and **freshly ground black pepper**

FOR THE QUINOA CAKES:

250g **quinoa**, cooked

1 **carrot**, grated

2 tablespoons **sesame seeds**

4 **spring onions**, finely chopped

2 tablespoons chopped **fresh parsley**

2 **eggs**

1 teaspoon **tamari**

FOR THE HOLLANDAISE:

3 **egg yolks** (room temperature)

1 tablespoon **water**

½ teaspoon **Dijon mustard**

½ teaspoon **wholegrain mustard**

150ml **olive oil** (not extra virgin)

1 tablespoon chopped **fresh tarragon**

1 tablespoon chopped **fresh chives**

lemon juice, to taste

1. Heat the oven to 100°C/250°F/gas mark ½.

2. Mix the quinoa cake ingredients together to form a thick batter. Season well and leave to one side.

3. Place a heatproof bowl over gently simmering water and whisk the egg yolks with the water and mustards to combine. Gently warm the oil in a separate pan so it is roughly the same temperature as the eggs – it should be lukewarm if you put your finger into the pan. Slowly drizzle the oil into the eggs, whisking after each addition until you have a thick emulsion. Add the herbs, lemon juice to taste and season well. Remove the pan from the heat, and the bowl from the simmering water, and set aside. Do not drain the water from the pan, as this can be used to blanch the asparagus and poach the eggs.

4. Heat the oil in a non-stick frying pan and drop large spoonfuls of the quinoa mix into the pan. You can make lots of small fritters or 4 large ones. Flatten with the back of a spoon and cook for 3 minutes on each side until browned and crisp. Place on a tray and keep warm in the very low-temperature oven.

5. Heat 1 tablespoon of olive oil in a large pan and tip in the spinach. Season well and stir vigorously until the spinach has wilted. Drain.

6. Blanch the asparagus in plenty of boiling water for 2 minutes. Drain and toss in a little olive oil. Season well and keep warm in the low oven.

7. Poach the eggs in simmering water for about 3 minutes. Remove from the pan and drain well.

8. To serve, top the quinoa cakes with spinach and asparagus. Place a poached egg on top and serve drizzled with the warm hollandaise.

Purple sprouting broccoli would also go well with this dish. If you want to make it paleo, swap the tamari for coconut aminos and the rice bran oil for olive oil.

COCONUT MANGO PANCAKES

These taste like an all-inclusive tropical honeymoon. In a nice clean way. These thin, crisp pancakes are also delightful with pineapple and banana.

PREP TIME: 10 MINS · COOK TIME: 10 MINS

50g **desiccated coconut**

50g **rice flour**

50g **cornflour**

1 **egg**

20ml **coconut milk**

100ml **water**

a pinch of **salt**

a drop of **vanilla extract**

25g **coconut sugar** or **palm sugar**

1 tablespoon **grapeseed oil**

1 **mango**

1. Cover the desiccated coconut with boiling water and set aside.

2. Sift the flours into a large bowl. Whisk together the egg, coconut milk and water. Add slowly to the flour until you have a thin batter. Add the salt and vanilla.

3. Drain the desiccated coconut and squeeze out any excess moisture. Heat a non-stick frying pan and dry toast the coconut over a medium heat with the sugar until it has caramelized slightly. Remove from the pan and wipe clean.

4. Heat the oil in the pan and add a small ladleful of the batter mix in the centre, tilting the pan to make a thin pancake. Cook for a minute on either side, then remove from the pan and repeat until you have used up all the batter and have a pile of pancakes.

5. Peel the mango and cut it into chunks or thin slices.

6. Serve each pancake with a little toasted coconut and mango.

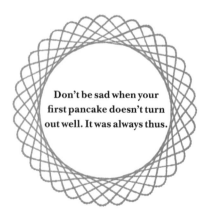

Don't be sad when your first pancake doesn't turn out well. It was always thus.

BUCKWHEAT CRÊPES

When first getting to grips with eating gluten-free, whether or not you can eat buckwheat always seems like a trick question. It is in fact, trick-free, gluten-free grass, and delightful served either savoury or sweet. We've served them here as a crêpe suzette – by segmenting a few blood oranges, sprinkling them with coconut sugar and finishing them off in the pan with a splash of Cointreau, but we'd also suggest serving them with cashew béchamel (see page 92) and cooked cabbage, or with the mushroom sauce from the lasagne (see page 174).

PREP TIME: 10 MINS · COOK TIME: 15 MINS

100g **buckwheat flour**

a pinch of **salt**

1 **egg**

300ml **almond milk**

2 teaspoons **pumpkin seed oil**

olive oil, for frying

blood oranges, to serve (see introduction, above)

1. Sieve the flour and salt into a bowl. Whisk the egg and add it to the with the pumpkin seed oil.

2. Slowly pour the wet ingredients into the dry, whisking until you have a smooth batter.

3. Heat a tablespoon of oil in a non-stick frying pan. Add a small ladleful of the batter and pour into the pan, tilting it so you have a thin layer over the pan surface. Cook for a minute, then flip the crêpe over and cook for another minute on the other side.

4. Repeat with the rest of the batter and serve with the blood oranges.

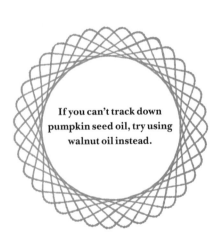

If you can't track down pumpkin seed oil, try using walnut oil instead.

GOOD MORNINGS

POHA

Poha is flattened, beaten or flaked rice; you can buy it in Asian and Indian supermarkets. If you can't find it, basmati rice will still be delicious. A traditional home-cooked Indian breakfast, its full flavour and fluffy lightness will fill you up for the day.

PREP TIME: 10 MINS · SOAK TIME: 15 MINS · COOK TIME: 15 MINS

100g **poha**

½ teaspoon **salt**

juice of ½ **lime**

½ teaspoon **ground turmeric**

½ teaspoon **chilli powder**

1 tablespoon **rice bran oil**

2 teaspoons **mustard seeds**

½ teaspoon **cumin seeds**

1 **red onion**, chopped

2 **green chillies**, chopped

10 **curry leaves**

1 **beefsteak tomato**, skinned, deseeded and chopped

1 **courgette**, chopped

2 tablespoons **flaked almonds**

salt and **freshly ground black pepper**

chopped **fresh coriander**, to serve

1. Rinse the poha in lots of cold water. Drain and cover with more water. Set aside for about 15 minutes, then drain again and break up any lumps. Add the salt, lime, turmeric and chilli, and mix well.

2. Heat the oil in a large pan. Add the mustard and cumin seeds, and, when they start to pop, tip in the onion, green chillies and curry leaves. Stir-fry until the onions start to brown.

3. Add the tomato and courgette. Cook for another 5 minutes, then add the poha and almonds. Stir-fry over a medium heat for another 5 minutes.

4. Check the seasoning and serve topped with chopped coriander.

You can buy poha online or in Asian shops. Jane likes the idea of rice being beaten with a blunt object.

BANAN-ALMOND PANCAKES

Don't let Pancake Day crêpe up on you – practise by eating pancakes way more often. Jane likes making these for her son. Jane likes her son. Even if he chucked a packet of Viennese biscuits at her for Mother's Day, only for her to find the empty packet of biscuits in his room later.

PREP TIME: 10 MINS
COOK TIME: 10 MINS

2 ripe **bananas**
1 **egg**
100ml **almond milk**
1 tablespoon **raw honey**, plus extra
   to serve
1 teaspoon **vanilla extract**
50g **almond flour**
100g **rice flour**
a pinch of **ground cinnamon**
1 teaspoon **baking powder**
a pinch of **bicarbonate of soda**
a pinch of **salt**
rapeseed oil, for frying

1. Blend the bananas with the egg, milk, honey and vanilla in a food processor, or mash well with a fork.

2. Sift together the dry ingredients in a large bowl. Slowly add the wet ingredients and whisk together until you have a thick batter.

3. Heat a tablespoon of oil in a large non-stick frying pan. Drop tablespoons of the batter into the pan and cook for 2 minutes on each side, until lightly browned on the outside.

4. Repeat until all the batter is used and serve drizzled with honey.

Serve with fresh berries, or any fruit that takes your fancy, and raw organic honey.

DEVON CRAB OMELETTE

|O| (4)

This tastes of a bright and peaceful morning in Koh Samui – or one of those smaller islands next door. It's a super-light omelette with a filling Pad Thai seasoning.

PREP TIME: 10 MINS · COOK TIME: 10 MINS

juice of 1 **lime**

2 tablespoons **fish sauce**, plus 2 teaspoons

1 tablespoon **palm sugar**

1 teaspoon **tamarind paste**

1 teaspoon **chilli sauce**

3 tablespoons **rice bran oil**

1 clove of **garlic**, crushed

6 **eggs**

a large pinch of **ground white pepper**

200g **white crabmeat**

50g **beansprouts**

a handful of **pea shoots**

½ **mooli**, julienned

50g **toasted peanuts**, chopped roughly

a small bunch of **chives**, cut into 2–3 cm lengths

2 tablespoons **fresh coriander leaves**

1. Mix together the lime juice, 2 tablespoons of fish sauce, the palm sugar, tamarind paste and chilli sauce to make your dressing. Set aside.

2. Heat 1 tablespoon of rice bran oil in a large non-stick frying pan or wok. Add the garlic to the pan and quickly stir-fry, then tip in the dressing. Bring to a simmer and cook for a few minutes, until the mixture has reduced and become syrupy. Take it off the heat and allow to cool.

3. Clean the pan, then heat the remaining oil. Whisk the eggs with the 2 teaspoons of fish sauce and the pepper. Pour half the eggs into the pan, tipping the pan to make a thin layer. Cook for 1 minute, then slide out on to a plate – do not turn it over. Repeat with the remaining egg mixture.

4. To serve, divide the crab between the omelettes and sprinkle with the beansprouts, pea shoots, mooli, peanuts and herbs. Drizzle with the syrupy dressing, fold the omelettes over, and slice each one in half to serve.

In the UK, we should eat more Devon crab. At the moment the bulk of it is exported, so get your hands on it before it goes.

SWEET POTATO QUESADILLAS WITH EGGS & AVOCADO

Let's start by clarifying that there's no queso in these dillas – but we challenge you to describe these tortilla packages any other way. We've used a combination of plain and blue corn tortillas here – we think they're beautiful. Your enjoyment of these should not be limited to breakfast, but it's a good place to start.

PREP TIME: 15 MINS · COOK TIME: 25 MINS

2 small **sweet potatoes** (or 1 large)

a pinch of **smoked paprika**

1 **shallot**, chopped

1 **green chilli**, chopped

2 tablespoons chopped **fresh coriander**, plus extra to serve

1 **cob of corn**, cooked and kernels removed

juice of 1 **lime**

2 **avocados**, roughly chopped

½ clove of **garlic**, crushed

3 tablespoons **olive oil**

8 small **corn tortillas** (see page 248)

4 **eggs**

salt and **cayenne pepper**

1. Heat the oven to 100°C/250°F/gas mark ½.

2. Peel the sweet potatoes and slice thinly, using a mandolin if you have one. Steam for about 15 minutes, until tender. Allow to cool, then fold through the paprika, shallot, chilli, coriander, cooked corn and half the lime juice. Season well.

3. Mix the avocados with the rest of the lime juice, garlic and 1 tablespoon of the olive oil. Season well.

4. Lay 4 corn tortillas on a clean surface. Spread the sweet potato mixture over the tortillas and top each with another tortilla.

5. Heat 1 tablespoon of oil in a non-stick frying pan and fry the tortillas one at a time for a minute on each side, being careful not to lose any filling when you flip them over. Transfer each tortilla to a tray in the low oven to keep warm. Alternatively, you can grill them for a minute on each side.

6. Fry the eggs in the leftover oil to your liking. To plate up, top each quesadilla with a fried egg and some of the avocado. Sprinkle with extra coriander to serve.

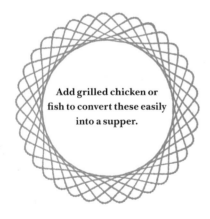

Add grilled chicken or fish to convert these easily into a supper.

1 **cauliflower**

500g **smoked haddock fillet**

2 tablespoons **rapeseed oil**

1 **onion**, finely chopped

2 **leeks**, sliced

a pinch of **saffron**

a pinch of **ground cardamom**

1 clove of **garlic**, crushed

1 × 2cm piece of **ginger**, grated

1 **red chilli**, chopped

1 teaspoon **curry powder**

2 teaspoons **nigella seeds**

100g **peas**, cooked

2 tablespoons chopped **fresh parsley**, plus extra to serve

4 **eggs**, boiled to your liking

2 tablespoons **flaked almonds**, toasted

salt and **freshly ground black pepper**

CAULI KEDGEREE

Now for a very British breakfast. We've made it with cauliflower couscous to pack more plants into your morning. Caul me, maybe?

PREP TIME: 15 MINS · COOK TIME: 25 MINS

1. Blitz the cauliflower florets in a food processor or on a fine grater until they resemble couscous.

2. Grill the fish for a few minutes until just cooked, then flake it into large pieces using 2 forks, or your hands.

3. Heat the oil in a large pan and cook the onion for 5 minutes over a low heat. Add the leeks, saffron and cardamom and cook for another 5 minutes before adding the garlic, ginger and chilli. Cook for 2 minutes, then tip in the cauliflower, curry powder and nigella seeds.

4. Stir well and cook for another 5 minutes, making sure the cauliflower doesn't stick. Fold in the peas, fish and chopped parsley and heat through.

5. Check the seasoning and serve garnished with the boiled eggs, toasted almonds and extra chopped parsley.

125g **split mung dal/beans**

200g **quinoa**

1 tablespoon **rice bran oil**

2 teaspoons **black mustard seeds**

2 teaspoons **crushed fennel seeds**

3 **cardamom pods**

1 × 2cm stick of **cinnamon**

½ teaspoon **ground cumin** and **coriander**

a pinch of **ground turmeric**

1 × 2cm piece of **ginger**, grated

1 litre **water** or **vegetable stock**

100g **peas**

100g **edamame beans**

100g **broad beans**

200g **courgettes**, diced

100g **spinach**, shredded

1 tablespoon chopped **fresh coriander**

salt and **freshly ground black pepper**

QUINOA KITCHARI

The inspiration for kedgeree (which sounds like a hungover Englishman trying to pronounce it) – this will soak up the sins of the night before.

PREP TIME: 10 MINS · SOAK TIME: OVERNIGHT
COOK TIME: 25 MINS

1. Soak the split dal overnight in plenty of cold water. Rinse the quinoa well. Drain both the dal and quinoa very well.

2. Heat the oil in a large saucepan and cook the spices for a minute, stirring well before tipping in the quinoa and dal. Cook for a minute, stirring well, and season. Add the stock. Bring up to a simmer and cook (covered) over a gentle heat for 15 minutes, until the quinoa is cooked through and the dal is soft.

3. Put the veg into a steamer, season, and leave for 5 minutes over a low heat to steam. Turn the heat off and fold the veg through the dal and quinoa. Cover and leave for 10 minutes.

4. Serve garnished with fresh coriander.

GOOD MORNINGS

ALMOND MILK PORRIDGE
WITH BANANA & CINNAMON

This porridge is just right. At Leon, we sell about 78,000 kilos of porridge a year. That's the equivalent of 40 elephants, 6 double-decker buses, or a Concorde. And just as fast.

PREP TIME: 5 MINS · COOK TIME: 10 MINS

100g **gluten-free oats**

500ml **unsweetened almond milk**

1 tablespoon **date and vanilla purée** (see below)

2–3 **bananas**

ground cinnamon, to garnish

1. Cook the oats with the almond milk in a small non-stick saucepan over a low heat, stirring very regularly for around 10 minutes, or until it has reached your desired consistency. We think it should be creamy, but not turn into mush.

2. Serve your porridge with a generous dollop of the date and vanilla purée, some sliced banana and a light dusting of cinnamon.

DATE & VANILLA PURÉE

PREP TIME: 5 MINS · MAKES A 200ML JAR

100g **medjool dates** (stones removed)

100ml **water**

seeds from 1 **vanilla pod**

1. Put all the ingredients into a blender and blitz until completely smooth.

2. This will make more than you need (roughly 10 portions), but it will keep fresh in your refrigerator for up to 7 days. It is also great spread on your nutty seedy loaf (see page 42).

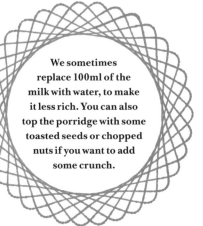

We sometimes replace 100ml of the milk with water, to make it less rich. You can also top the porridge with some toasted seeds or chopped nuts if you want to add some crunch.

TRUFFLE-CODDLED EGGS

A luxurious Sunday morning treat. Totally worth the truffle.
Thank you to our friend Brad for the inspiration.

PREP TIME: 20 MINS · COOK TIME: 35 MINS

200g **Jerusalem artichokes**

2 tablespoons **olive oil**

100g **chestnut mushrooms**, sliced

½ clove of **garlic**, crushed

leaves from 1 sprig of **fresh thyme**

50g **kale**, cooked

4 **eggs**

1 tablespoon chopped **fresh chives**

a drizzle of **truffle oil**

salt and **freshly ground black pepper**

1. Heat the oven to 180°C/350°F/gas mark 4.

2. Peel the Jerusalem artichokes and slice them thinly. Heat 1 tablespoon of oil in a small pan and add the artichokes. Cook for a few minutes over a high heat. Season well and cover. Lower the heat and leave to cook gently for about 10 minutes, or until they are soft. Blitz until smooth with a hand blender or in a food processor and set aside.

3. Heat the rest of the oil in a frying pan. Cook the mushrooms with the garlic and thyme for 5 minutes, until they have softened. Season well.

4. Chop the kale and season well.

5. Take 4 ramekins and divide the kale between them. Top with the mushrooms and finish with the artichoke purée. Make an indentation in the purée and crack an egg into each ramekin. Sprinkle with salt and pepper.

6. Place the ramekins in a baking tray and pour in boiling water so that it comes three-quarters up the side of the ramekins. This makes a water bath, and ensures that everything cooks evenly and doesn't become rubbery. Transfer (carefully) to the oven and bake for about 15–20 minutes, depending on how you like your eggs cooked.

7. Remove from the oven and sprinkle with the chopped chives and truffle oil before serving.

If Jerusalem artichokes aren't in season (and you're not veggie), try the cauliflower and anchovy purée (see page 78).

SMASHED BROAD BEANS, KALE & HAM

You can make this recipe with shredded ham, but by cooking the ham hock you get a better result plus some extra stock to make soup. I think, therefore I ham.

PREP TIME: 15 MINS · SOAK TIME: 1 HOUR · COOK TIME: 1 HOUR

1 **ham hock**

vegetables for stock (**onion, celery, leek, carrot**, trimmings)

1 **onion**, chopped

2 tablespoons **olive oil**

200g **broad beans** (frozen are fine)

1 clove of **garlic**, thinly sliced

a pinch of **chilli flakes**

100g **kale**, cooked and chopped

4 **eggs**

white wine vinegar

1 tablespoon shredded **fresh mint**

salt and **freshly ground black pepper**

1 tablespoon chopped **fresh parsley**, to serve

a drizzle of **olive oil**, to serve

1. Soak the ham hock in cold water for an hour. Drain and place in a pressure cooker with some stock vegetables added, for example onion, celery, leek and carrot trimmings (or just use vegetable stock).

2. Bring up to steam and cook over a medium heat for 40 minutes. This step can be done in a normal pan but will take over 3 hours.

3. Allow the ham hock to cool down in the stock. Drain, reserving the cooking liquor. Shred about 150g of the ham hock meat and set aside. The rest of the ham will keep in the refrigerator for up to 4 days.

4. Cook the onion in a little oil for 10 minutes, until soft. Add the broad beans and stir well to combine. Add 400ml of the ham stock and simmer for 5 minutes, or until the beans are soft. Place half the mix in a food processor and blitz to chop roughly. Return to the pan and fold together with the rest of the beans. Season with black pepper.

5. Heat the rest of the oil in a small pan. Add the garlic and chilli flakes and cook for 2 minutes, until fragrant but without colouring. Add the chopped kale and braise together for 2 minutes. Fold in the reserved 150g of shredded ham hock.

6. Poach the eggs in plenty of simmering water containing a good slug of vinegar for about 4 minutes. Drain on kitchen paper.

7. Fold the mint through the broad beans, then on each plate place a little of the smashed beans and braised kale. Top with a poached egg and sprinkle with parsley and a drizzle of olive oil to serve.

HIP HOPPERS
WITH FOUR TOPPERS

This Sri Lankan fermented rice batter makes enough for 8 egg hoppers (2 each) plus a few extra pancakes. You have to start this recipe the day before, so the batter has time to develop or ferment. The hoppers are traditionally cooked in special small high-sided pans, but a deep small non-stick pan will do. As with pancakes, the first few may not work. Do persevere, and we find that they cook better on a gas stove where the heat goes up the sides of the pan. Any (or all) of the accompaniments overleaf are great with the hoppers. Hop to it.

PREP TIME: 15 MINS · STAND TIME: OVERNIGHT · COOK TIME: 2–3 MINS EACH

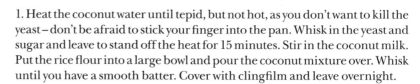

50ml **coconut water**

½ teaspoon **dried yeast**

½ teaspoon **coconut sugar**

150ml **coconut milk**

100g **brown rice flour**

50ml, plus extra **soda water**

a large pinch of **salt**

rapeseed oil

8 **eggs**

1. Heat the coconut water until tepid, but not hot, as you don't want to kill the yeast – don't be afraid to stick your finger into the pan. Whisk in the yeast and sugar and leave to stand off the heat for 15 minutes. Stir in the coconut milk. Put the rice flour into a large bowl and pour the coconut mixture over. Whisk until you have a smooth batter. Cover with clingfilm and leave overnight.

2. In the morning, add the soda water and whisk well. Season with salt. Leave to stand for an hour before using – it should be thinner than a traditional pancake batter. If it has thickened on standing, or if your coconut milk was very thick, add some extra soda water until it is the consistency of single cream.

3. Heat your pan and pour some oil into a bowl. Dip a clean cloth into the oil and use it to rub around the pan. Slowly pour a small ladleful of the batter into the pan, tilting it so the batter coats up the edges of the pan and is distributed in a thin layer. Quickly crack an egg into the base of the pan over the hopper and cover. Leave to cook for about 2 minutes, or until the egg is just cooked and the edges of the pancake are starting to brown. Run around the edges with a palette knife and ease on to a plate to serve.

4. Repeat with the remaining batter and eggs. Any extra can be saved or cooked plain without eggs.

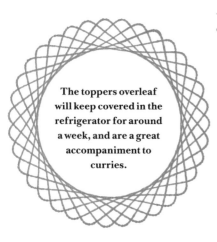

The toppers overleaf will keep covered in the refrigerator for around a week, and are a great accompaniment to curries.

COCONUT GRAVY

1 **onion**, sliced

2 cloves of **garlic**, crushed

½ teaspoon **ground turmeric**

½ teaspoon **ground fenugreek seeds**

1 × 2.5cm stick of **cinnamon**

3 **green chillies**, roughly chopped

10 **curry leaves**

400ml **coconut milk**

juice of ½ **lime**

salt

PREP TIME: 5 MINS · COOK TIME: 15 MINS
ENOUGH FOR 8 HOPPERS

1. Place all the ingredients, apart from the lime juice and salt, in a pan. Put over a medium heat and bring up to a simmer. Cook gently for about 15 minutes, or until the onions have softened and the gravy has thickened.

2. Season well and add lime juice to taste.

GREEN SAMBAL

3 tablespoons **desiccated coconut**

2 tablespoons chopped **fresh parsley**

a handful of de-stemmed **kale**, finely shredded

2 large **shallots**, finely chopped

3 **green chillies**, finely chopped

1 tablespoon **lime juice**

salt

PREP TIME: 5 MINS · STAND TIME: 15 MINS
ENOUGH FOR 8 HOPPERS

1. Cover the coconut with boiling water and leave to stand for about 15 minutes. Place in a sieve and lightly press to remove excess water.

2. Mix with the other ingredients in a bowl and season well.

SEENI SAMBAL

2 tablespoons **rice bran oil**

1 × 2 cm stick of **cinnamon**

2 **cloves**

3 **cardamom pods**, crushed

3 **red onions**, finely chopped

2 sprigs of **fresh curry leaves**

1 tablespoon **red chilli flakes**

2 teaspoons **palm sugar**

1 teaspoon **tamarind paste**

salt and **freshly ground black pepper**

PREP TIME: 5 MINS · COOK TIME: 20 MINS
ENOUGH FOR 8 HOPPERS

1. Heat the oil in a large pan. Add the cinnamon, cloves and cardamom pods. Cook for a minute, stirring. Add the onions, curry leaves and red chilli flakes and cook for 10 minutes over a low heat without browning them.

2. Stir in the sugar and tamarind paste and mix well. Cook slowly for another 10 minutes, adding a little water if the onions start to stick. Season well.

LUNU MIRIS

1 large **red onion**, finely chopped

2 tablespoons **red chilli flakes**

2 **red chillies**, finely chopped

1 tablespoon **lime juice**

salt

PREP TIME: 5 MINS
ENOUGH FOR 8 HOPPERS

1. Mix the chopped onion with the dried and fresh chillies. Pound them together in a pestle and mortar (or give them a quick pulse in a food processor).

2. Place in a bowl and mix with the lime juice and salt.

Use an ice-cream scoop to get perfectly even muffins. Raspberries would work very well here too.

BLUEBERRY MUFFINS

A little bit of berried treasure to discover at breakfast. They're so easy to make, there's really muffin to it. This is a recipe from our friends Meleni and Rob from the Alliance of Natural Health.

PREP TIME: 10 MINS · COOK TIME: 20 MINS

100g **coconut oil**, melted, plus extra for greasing

4 **eggs**, whisked

1 teaspoon **vanilla extract**

100g **rice malt syrup**

85ml **almond milk**

200g **almond flour**

2 teaspoons **baking powder**

½ teaspoon **salt**

100g **blueberries** (frozen are fine if fresh aren't in season)

1. Heat the oven to 180°C/350°F/gas mark 4.

2. Grease a muffin tray and put it to one side, or line the tray with paper muffin cups if you prefer. Sieve all the dry ingredients and mix together.

3. Whisk the wet ingredients together and stir into the dry.

4. Fold through the blueberries. Add a tablespoon of mixture to each section of the muffin tray and cook in the oven for about 15–20 minutes, or until a skewer comes out clean. Leave to cool before serving.

NUTTY SEEDY LOAF

Be the breadwinner with this loaf. It makes great toast, and keeps for about a week. Flax seeds, chia seeds and psyllium husks help the dough to stretch and mimic the properties of gluten. Jane came up with this recipe and when she shared it, John was excited to see that it was very similar to a recipe that his friends Louka and Wendy had made for him on their trip to Lamu. So this is dedicated to Wendy and Louka, two of the wisest people John knows.

PREP TIME: 10 MINS · CHILLING TIME: OVERNIGHT · COOK TIME: 1 HOUR 10 MINS

50g **pumpkin seeds**

50g **sunflower seeds**

50g **sesame seeds**

100g **almond flour**

100g **buckwheat flour**

100g **gluten-free oats**

50g **flaxseeds**

2 tablespoons **ground psyllium husks**

2 tablespoons **ground chia seeds**

50ml **olive oil**

2 tablespoons **rice malt syrup**

500ml **water**

1 teaspoon **salt**

1. Heat the oven to 170°C/350°F/gas mark 3.

2. Place the pumpkin, sunflower and sesame seeds on a baking tray and toast for 10 minutes, until lightly browned. Place in a bowl and allow to cool. Mix with the 2 flours, oats, flaxseeds, psyllium and chia seeds.

3. Mix the wet ingredients with the salt and whisk to blend together. Pour into the dry ingredients and beat with a spoon to make sure everything is mixed together thoroughly.

4. Pour the mixture into a 23 × 13cm loaf tin lined with baking parchment tin and flatten down with the back of a spoon. Cover, and leave to rest overnight in the refrigerator.

5. Heat the oven to 200°C/400°F/gas mark 6. Take the tin out of the refrigerator and allow the loaf to come up to room temperature. Bake in the oven for an hour, then place on a cooling rack and leave to cool completely before turning out. The loaf will keep well in a sealed container and is fab toasted and spread with soya spread.

2

FOR STARTERS

PUFFED RICE
WITH PORK & PRAWN DIP

Posh rice cakes with a rich satay-style sauce. Make a few extra bunches of puffed rice and top them with almond butter and bananas for breakfast. The trick to making the puffed rice pieces hold their shape is to really squash the rice down. Putting a sheet of greaseproof, or cling film over the top stops your hands getting sticky and let's you really go for it until it's super compact.

PREP TIME: 15 MINS · COOK TIME: 1 HOUR, 10 MINS

200g **jasmine rice**

500ml **water**

salt

1 tablespoon **coconut oil**

150g **minced pork**

150g **raw prawn meat**, chopped

2 **shallots**, finely chopped

1 tablespoon chopped **coriander stalks**

1 clove of **garlic**, crushed

2 teaspoons **ground white pepper**

2 tablespoons **fish sauce**

2 teaspoons **tamarind paste**

1 tablespoon **palm sugar**

250ml **coconut milk**

50g **roasted peanuts**, ground

1 teaspoon **fish paste** (**balachan**)

rice bran oil, for frying

salt and **freshly ground black pepper**

1. Put the rice and water into a pan together along with a pinch of salt. Bring to the boil, then turn the heat down and simmer for about 20 minutes, until all the water has been absorbed.

2. Tip the rice on to a baking tray lined with greaseproof paper. Place another sheet of greaseproof on top and press down firmly until you have a thin layer of rice. Remove the top sheet and cut the rice into small squares with a knife. Allow to cool. Dry the rice out in a heated very low oven (90°C/190°F/lowest gas mark) for about 30 minutes. Flip the squares over and return them to the oven until completely dry. Keep in a sealed container until needed.

3. Heat the coconut oil in a large frying pan. Fry the pork until lightly browned. Remove with a slotted spoon. Fry the prawn meat for a few minutes and add to the pork. Cook the shallots with the coriander, garlic and pepper for a few minutes. Blitz the pork and prawns in a food processor, then return to the pan and stir well over a low heat for 5 minutes. Add the fish sauce, tamarind, sugar and coconut milk. Bring the mixture up to a simmer and cook gently for 5 minutes. Stir in the peanuts and fish paste and season well.

4. Heat some oil in a pan (about 2cm deep). Fry the rice cakes in batches until puffed and golden brown. Serve with the pork and prawn dip.

OKA(Y)

4

500g **gurnard** or **bream fillets**,
pin-boned and skinned, cut into
1–2cm chunks

juice of 4 **limes**

2 large **tomatoes**, skinned,
deseeded and cut into fine dice

4 **spring onions,** finely chopped

1 small **red onion**, finely chopped

1 **red chilli**, chopped

½ **cucumber**, peeled, deseeded
and finely chopped

300ml **coconut cream**

2 tablespoons chopped **fresh
coriander**

salt and **freshly ground black
pepper**

Oka is a Samoan variation of poke that you can buy as a street snack served in a plastic cup. Bill and Ross gave Jane this recipe from their restaurant, Bistro Tatau, where Jane worked while she was pregnant.

PREP TIME: 15 MINS · CURE TIME: 20 MINS

1. Place the fish in a glass bowl and cover with the lime juice. Sprinkle with salt and leave for 20 minutes to 'cook'.

2. Drain the fish and mix with the diced and chopped vegetables in a large bowl. Fold in the coconut cream and season well.

3. Serve in a glass bowl or a plastic cup and top with the chopped coriander.

HOKEY POKE

6

500g **salmon** (or **tuna**) **fillet**

2 teaspoons **sesame oil**

2 teaspoons finely grated **ginger**

2 teaspoons **tamari**

1 **red chilli**, deseeded and finely
chopped

1 tablespoon **toasted sesame
seeds**

½ **kohlrabi**, cut into fine strips (or
julienne)

1 bunch of **spring onions**, cut into
strips

coriander leaves, to garnish

2 teaspoons **black sesame seeds**,
to serve

You do the hokey-poke, and you turn around. That's what it's all about. This Hawaiian dish is traditionally made with very fresh yellowfin tuna, but salmon is a good substitute.

PREP TIME: 15 MINS

1. Cut the fish into 1–2cm chunks.

2. Mix together the sesame oil, ginger, tamari, chilli and toasted sesame seeds and toss the fish in the marinade.

3. Sprinkle the kohlrabi and spring onions on a serving dish. Place the fish with the marinade on top and scatter with the coriander leaves and black sesame seeds to serve.

Any firm
white-fleshed fish
can be used in this dish.
It also works well with the
fruity addition of 300g ripe,
sliced papaya at the bottom
of the serving cup.

PRAWN SUMMER ROLLS

These make a punchy and aromatic starter, or a tidy snack for a summer picnic. Prawn to be wild.

PREP TIME: 35 MINS

50g **vermicelli rice noodles**

1 teaspoon **sesame oil**

8 **lettuce leaves**

basil and **mint leaves** – about 24 (3 for each roll)

8 sprigs of **coriander**

16 **cooked king prawns**

8 **rice paper wrappers**

ALL CUT INTO FINE STRIPS

1 **carrot**

½ **red pepper**

¼ **cucumber**

6 **sugar snaps**

¼ **mooli** or **kohlrabi**

1. Cover the noodles with boiling water for about 2 minutes, or until they are al dente. Drain and refresh. Cut into smaller pieces and toss in sesame oil.

2. Lay out the lettuce leaves and top each one with the herbs, strips of veg and a little of the noodles. Top each one with 2 prawns.

3. Soak one rice paper wrapper in warm water until soft and pliable. Place on a damp cloth and top with one of the filled lettuce leaves, then roll up as tightly as possible, folding in the sides to make a parcel. Repeat with the rest of the wrappers.

4. To serve, slice each roll in half diagonally and serve with nuoc cham dipping sauce (see below).

NUOC CHAM DIPPING SAUCE

PREP TIME: 15 MINS · COOK TIME: 5 MINS · COOL TIME: 5 MINS

1 tablespoon **rice vinegar**

1 tablespoon **palm sugar**

2 tablespoons **water**

2 **red chillies**, deseeded and finely chopped

1 clove of **garlic**, crushed

2 tablespoons **fish sauce** (or **tamari** for veggies)

juice of 1 **lime**

coriander leaves

1. In a saucepan, bring the vinegar, palm sugar and water to the boil. Allow to cool, then add the rest of the dipping sauce ingredients. This will keep in a sealed container in the refrigerator for up to 4 days.

These also work well if you make them completely vegetarian, or use duck, pork or rare beef. If you want a lighter option, use shredded mooli or kohlrabi instead of the noodles.

FOUR-STYLE CURED SALMON

In search of a cure for salmon, we made these four. Fancy a fifth? Try serving it with the hollandaise on page 16 for an eggs royale worthy of the Queen. Below is how to cure the salmon, and opposite are our suggestions for how to enjoy it.

PREP TIME: 5 MINS · CURE TIME: 2 DAYS

500g piece of **salmon**, skin on, pin-boned

3 tablespoons **sea salt**

2 tablespoons **raw honey**

2 tablespoons **Sambuca** or other **aniseed liqueur** (optional)

2 tablespoons chopped **fresh dill**

1 teaspoon **ground white pepper**

1. Cut the salmon in half horizontally. Mix the salt with the honey, Sambuca, dill and pepper and spread over the flesh of the salmon halves. Sandwich the pieces together and wrap in clingfilm. Place in a non-reactive dish with a weight on top. This could be a tin or anything that will apply a little pressure to the salmon.

2. Place in the refrigerator for about 36 hours, turning every 8 hours. Remove from the clingfilm and wipe with kitchen paper. To serve, slice the salmon thinly.

1.

2.

3.

4.

1. CUCUMBER & DILL SALAD WITH MUSTARD SAUCE

PREP TIME: 10 MINS · SALT TIME: 30 MINS

1 **cucumber**, peeled and deseeded

1 tablespoon **cider vinegar**, plus 2 teaspoons

1 teaspoon **coconut sugar**

2 tablespoons chopped **fresh chives**

1 tablespoon **Dijon mustard**

1 tablespoon **raw honey**

1 tablespoon finely chopped **fresh dill**

2 tablespoons **grapeseed oil**

cured salmon, thinly sliced (see left)

1 bunch of **watercress**

salt

1. Slice the cucumber into thin strips. Sprinkle with salt and leave in a colander for about 30 minutes. Pat dry and toss with 2 teaspoons of the cider vinegar, the sugar and chives.

2. Blend together the mustard, honey, dill, oil and remaining 1 tablespoon of vinegar.

3. To serve, arrange the salmon to one side of each plate and drizzle with the dressing. Pile up the cucumber salad to one side, with some of the watercress.

2. CHICORY, CELERIAC & CAPERS

PREP TIME: 15 MINS · SOAK TIME: 20 MINS

2 heads of **red chicory**

200g **celeriac**, peeled and grated

1 tablespoon **olive oil**

1 teaspoon **fresh tarragon**, finely chopped

cured salmon, thinly sliced (see left)

2 tablespoons **capers**, soaked for about 20 minutes

1 small **red onion**, thinly sliced

1. Separate the leaves from the chicory and arrange on a plate. Toss the celeriac with the oil and tarragon, and sprinkle over the chicory.

2. Top with salmon, capers and red onion and serve.

3. BEETROOT & BUCKWHEAT BLINIS WITH HORSERADISH

PREP TIME: 15 MINS · COOL TIME: 5 MINS

1 large **beetroot**, peeled and grated

1 tablespoon **olive oil**

2 teaspoons **caraway seeds**

juice 1 **orange**

8 **buckwheat blinis** (see page 70)

cured salmon, thinly sliced (see left)

1 tablespoon chopped **fresh chives**

4 **radishes**, sliced and cut into thin needles

1 × 5cm piece of **fresh horseradish**, peeled

salt and **freshly ground black pepper**

1. Place the beetroot in a bowl. Heat the oil in a small pan, then add the caraway seeds and stir and cook for a minute. Add the orange juice, turn up the heat and reduce the juice to a thick syrup, this should take a couple of minutes. Dress the beetroot with the syrup, season well and allow to cool.

2. Top each blini with a little beetroot and salmon. Sprinkle with the chives and radishes. Finally, grate fresh horseradish over all the blinis to serve.

4. FENNEL, CELERY, & PINK PEPPERCORNS

PREP TIME: 10 MINS

cured salmon, thinly sliced (see left)

½ head of **fennel**, thinly sliced

1 **celery heart**, thinly sliced

2 teaspoons crushed **pink peppercorns**

a drizzle of **olive oil**

celery leaves

1. Arrange the salmon on a large plate and sprinkle over the fennel, celery and peppercorns.

2. Drizzle with olive oil and scatter over the celery leaves to serve.

MUSSEL & COURGETTE FRITTERS

(✓)
(P)
(SF)

You can buy cooked mussel meat either fresh or frozen, or of course, you could cook your own.

PREP TIME: 20 MINS · STAND TIME: 20 MINS · COOK TIME: 10 MINS

1 **courgette**, grated

½ teaspoon **salt**

250g **cooked mussel meat**

1 bunch of **spring onions**, chopped

2 tablespoons chopped **fresh chives**

zest of 1 **lemon**

2 **eggs**

2 tablespoons **almond flour**

a pinch of **cayenne pepper**

olive oil, for frying

a bunch of **watercress**

freshly ground black pepper

RED PEPPER SAUCE

100g **piquillo peppers** or peeled **red peppers**

1 clove of **garlic**, crushed

1 **red chilli**, chopped

2 tablespoons **olive oil**

salt and **freshly ground black pepper**

1. Place the grated courgette in a colander and sprinkle with the salt. Set aside for at least 20 minutes.

2. Place the mussel meat in a food processor and blitz for a few seconds so the mussels are roughly chopped (this can be done by hand). Tip out into a large bowl.

3. Add the rest of the ingredients to the processor and blitz briefly until combined. Empty into the bowl of mussels.

4. Squeeze out the liquid from the grated courgettes and add to the bowl. Fold everything together and check the seasoning.

5. Make the sauce by blending the peppers with the garlic, chilli and oil. Season to taste.

6. To cook the fritters, heat a few tablespoons of oil in a large non-stick frying pan. Drop tablespoons of the mixture into the oil, pressing each one down to make a fritter about ½–1cm deep. Cook for 2 minutes on each side. After each batch is cooked, transfer to a plate and keep warm.

7. To serve, place a few fritters on each plate with a spoonful of the pepper sauce and some watercress.

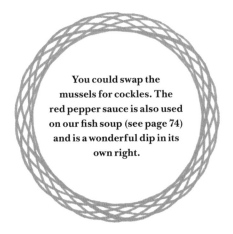

You could swap the mussels for cockles. The red pepper sauce is also used on our fish soup (see page 74) and is a wonderful dip in its own right.

SQUASHED CORN CAKES

·:8:·

NF
V
SF

It will be very tempting to coat everything in tortilla chips after trying this recipe. These would also make a smashing breakfast patty, served with fried eggs and salsa.

PREP TIME: 25 MINS · CURE TIME: 50 MINS

500g **butternut squash**, cut into small dice

2 tablespoons **olive oil**

1 **red onion**, chopped

1 clove of **garlic**, crushed

1 **red chilli**, chopped

a pinch of **ground turmeric**

a pinch of **ground cumin**

100g **piquillo peppers** or peeled **red peppers**, chopped

2 **cobs of corn**, kernels only

2 tablespoons **tomato passata**

100g **cannellini beans**

100g **kidney beans**

olive oil, for frying

avocado, lime and coriander salsa, to serve

salt and **freshly ground black pepper**

FOR THE COATING

4 tablespoons **rice flour**

2 **eggs,** beaten

1 small pack of **tortilla chips**, crushed

1. Heat the oven to 180°C/350°F/gas mark 4.

2. Toss the squash pieces in 1 tablespoon of oil and season well. Place on a baking tray and roast in the oven for about 30 minutes, until the squash is tender. Remove from the oven.

3. While the squash is cooking, heat the remaining oil in a large frying pan and cook the onion for 5 minutes over a medium heat without allowing it to colour. Add the garlic and spices and cook for another minute. Tip in the cooked squash along with the peppers, corn and passata. Stir well and cook for 5 minutes.

4. Drain the beans and rinse well. Place half in a food processor and blitz for a few seconds to chop them roughly (this can also be done by hand). Stir all the beans, chopped and unchopped, into the squash mix, season well, then empty into a bowl and leave to cool down.

5. Once cool, shape the mixture into 8 small cakes. Coat each one first with rice flour, then with beaten egg and finally with crushed tortilla chips. Place on a tray in the refrigerator to firm up before frying – about an hour.

6. Heat the oil to about 1cm deep in a non-stick frying pan. Cook the squash cakes for about 4 minutes on each side, until lightly browned. Drain on kitchen paper and serve with avocado, lime and coriander salsa (see page 214), if liked.

These are great served with an avocado, lime and coriander salsa (see tip, page 214).

GAJAK SNACKS

This is an assortment of Mauritian street food snacks. Perfect for a summer street party.

1. BOULETTES

These can be served in a chicken broth with chopped spring onions or with hot chilli sauce. You can buy chayote in most African or West Indian shops – they're green and look a bit like a green backside. They're also referred to as chowchow, so chow down.

PREP TIME: 5 MINS · COOK TIME: 20 MINS

350g grated **chayote, kohlrabi** or **mooli**
a pinch of **salt**
175g **raw prawns**, chopped
1 tablespoon **tamari**
1 teaspoon finely grated **ginger**
about 25g **tapioca starch**
chopped **chives**, to serve

1. Place the grated chayote in a colander and sprinkle with a little salt. Leave for 20 minutes, then place in a clean tea towel and squeeze out any excess water.

2. Place the chayote in a bowl with the prawns, tamari and grated ginger. Stir in the tapioca starch a spoonful at a time, until all the ingredients are coated and the mixture comes together – this may not require the full 25g.

3. Shape the dough into balls about 3cm in diameter and place in a steamer. Steam for 15–20 minutes. Serve scattered with chives.

2. GATEAU PIMENTS

These little hot, crispy dal fritters are sort of like falafel. Except they're not.

PREP TIME: 10 MINS · COOK TIME: 5 MINS
SOAK TIME: OVERNIGHT

200g **yellow split peas**, soaked overnight in lots of cold water
1 teaspoon **bicarbonate of soda**
1 teaspoon **ground cumin**
2 tablespoons chopped **fresh coriander**
4 **spring onions**, chopped
2 **shallots**, chopped
½ teaspoon **ground turmeric**
3 **green chillies**, chopped
rapeseed oil, for deep- or shallow-frying
salt and **freshly ground black pepper**

1. Drain the split peas well. Tip them into a food processor with all the other ingredients except for the oil, and blitz until well combined but not completely smooth. Season.

2. Heat the oil for frying. Shape the mixture into small flattened discs and fry for a few minutes until lightly browned all over. Drain on kitchen paper before serving.

1.

2.

3.

♥ NF V Ve SF

3. CABBAGE BHAJIS

PREP TIME: 5 MINS · COOK TIME: 8 MINS

100g **gram flour**
½ teaspoon **baking powder**
about 100ml **soda water**
200g **cabbage**, grated
1 teaspoon **ground turmeric**
a pinch of **cayenne pepper**
6 **spring onions**, chopped
1 **green chilli**, chopped
2 tablespoons chopped **fresh
    coriander**
1 teaspoon **ground cumin**
rapeseed oil, for frying
salt and **freshly ground black
    pepper**

1. Mix the flour with the baking powder and add soda water until you have a thick batter.

2. Add the rest of the ingredients, except for the oil, and mix well. The batter should just coat the cabbage. Season.

3. Heat the oil for frying, and deep-fry the bhajis at 180°C for a few minutes until browned and crisp. Drain on kitchen paper before serving.

ALMOND & MELON SOUP

Soaking the almonds in the water overnight gives them a better flavour. Best served totally chilled, this Spanish-inspired soup is one in a melon.

PREP TIME: 15 MINS · SOAK TIME: OVERNIGHT

200g **whole blanched almonds**

800ml **cold water**

3 cloves of **garlic**, crushed

3 tablespoons **sherry vinegar**

½ **cucumber**, peeled and chopped

200g **melon flesh** (such as **cantaloupe**)

150ml good-quality **extra virgin olive oil**

salt and **ground white pepper**

TO SERVE

toasted almonds

a drizzle of **olive oil**

seedless **green grapes**, sliced (optional)

melon, diced (optional)

1. The night before making the soup, soak the almonds in half the water.

2. Mix the almonds and the remaining fresh water in a large bowl with the garlic, vinegar, cucumber and melon. Stir everything together well. Using a liquidizer, blend together in batches (you don't want it all over the ceiling), adding some of the olive oil to each batch until smooth. Season well.

3. If the soup is too thick, add a little water or more olive oil to get it to the required consistency. Pass the soup through the fine blade of a food mill (mouli-légumes).

4. Put the soup into the refrigerator for at least 2 hours. Sprinkle with the almonds and oil to garnish and serve with the grapes and melon on the side, if liked. Do not try to garnish with the grapes and melon – they don't float (we learned that the hard way).

The amount of garlic can be reduced if preferred. You could also serve the soup with a few ice cubes in it if you like it really chilled.

SPICED SPINACH, PEA & POTATO CAKES

Gram flour gives an epic crunch to these protein-packed patties. They work really well with the kachumber salad (see page 254) or any of the sambals from the hoppers toppers (see page 40).

PREP TIME: 5 MINS · COOK TIME: 20 MINS

2 tablespoons **gram flour**, plus extra for dusting

50g **spinach**, cooked

200g **potatoes**, mashed

100g **peas**

1 **green chilli**, chopped

1 teaspoon finely grated **ginger**

2 tablespoons **coriander**, chopped

a pinch of **ground turmeric**

a pinch of **ground cardamom**

a pinch of **garam masala**

rapeseed oil, for frying

salt and **freshly ground black pepper**

1. Dry-fry the gram flour until lightly toasted. Place in a large bowl. Squeeze out any excess moisture from the spinach, season and chop. Add to the gram flour along with the rest of the ingredients except for the oil. Season and mix together well.

2. Shape into small cakes and dust with a little gram flour. Shallow-fry in a little oil for 3 minutes on each side, or until lightly browned. Drain on kitchen paper before serving.

FOR STARTERS

Serve topped with smoked or cured salmon (see page 52), or as we've done here with some cooked prawns with a dill mayonnaise.

PUMPKIN LATKES

This recipe is all about substitution. If pumpkins are not in season, use squash, or swap cassava for parsnips, taro or sweet potatoes. When you've made these once, you'll be making them a latke.

PREP TIME: 20 MINS · COOK TIME: 10 MINS

300g **pumpkin flesh**, grated

300g **casava**, grated

½ teaspoon **salt**

6 **spring onions**, chopped

½ teaspoon **ground turmeric**

1 tablespoon **mustard seeds**

1 tablespoon chopped **fresh dill**

1 **egg**, beaten

1 tablespoon **gram flour**

rapeseed oil, for frying

freshly ground black pepper

1. Place the grated veg in a colander over a bowl and sprinkle with salt. Leave for about 30 minutes. Press down on the grated veg with the back of a large spoon to push out any excess moisture. Transfer to a large bowl.

2. Add the rest of the ingredients except for the oil, and mix together well.

3. Heat some oil in a non-stick frying pan. Drop spoonfuls of the mix into the oil and cook for 2 minutes on each side, until golden brown and crisp. Drain on kitchen paper before serving.

SPICY DAL CAKE

This spicy, savoury lentil cake is also known as ondhwo or handvo. When Jane was at uni in Leeds, she worked in an Indian restaurant called Hansa's, and this is based on a recipe she learned there.

PREP TIME: 15 MINS · FERMENTING TIME: OVERNIGHT
COOK TIME: 35 MINS

120g **rice flour**

100g **lentil/dal flour**

200ml **warm water**

400g **sugar-free coconut yoghurt**

1½ teaspoons **salt**

½ teaspoon **ground turmeric**

2 **green chillies**, deseeded and chopped

100g **sweetcorn kernels**, cooked and chopped

1 **sweet potato**, peeled and finely chopped

2 **carrots**, grated

2 **onions**, finely chopped

2 teaspoons **bicarbonate of soda**

3 tablespoons **rapeseed oil**

1 tablespoon **black mustard seeds**

1 tablespoon **cumin seeds**

3 tablespoons chopped **fresh coriander**

5 tablespoons **sesame seeds**

1. Heat the oven to 200°C/400°F/gas mark 6.

2. Sift the rice flour and dal flour together in a large bowl. Whisk in the warm water, yoghurt, salt, turmeric and chillies. Cover and leave at room temperature to ferment overnight (about 12 hours).

3. Add all the chopped and grated vegetables to the mix along with the bicarbonate of soda. Line a baking tray about 28cm wide and quite deep with baking parchment and spoon the mix into the tray.

4. Heat the oil in a frying pan and fry the mustard and cumin seeds until the mustard seeds pop. Stir in the coriander and cook for 2 minutes, then spread on top of the mix in the baking tray. Sprinkle with the sesame seeds – it should resemble a crust.

5. Bake in the oven for about 30 minutes, or until a skewer comes out clean. Allow to cool for 30 minutes, then cut into squares and serve as a starter or a side with chutneys.

SAUSAGE ROLLS

Jane's son ate the whole lot when she made these at home. For the ultimate pub grub, forget everything you think you know about lard. It's natural, unlike the polyunsaturates found in vegetable oil (but remember it works better in savoury recipes). Roll with it. This pastry is particularly crumbly due to the lack of gluten, so it may be a little tricky to roll out, but don't panic if it cracks – just cover the cracks with plenty of egg wash before it goes in the oven.

PREP TIME: 20 MINS · REST TIME: 15 MINS · COOK TIME: 40 MINS

1 tablespoon **olive oil**

1 **onion**, chopped

1 **leek**, finely chopped

3 sticks of **celery**, finely chopped

1 clove of **garlic**, crushed

400g good-quality **sausage meat**

1 **apple**, peeled and grated

2 teaspoons **wholegrain mustard**

2 teaspoons **Dijon mustard**

2 teaspoons **gluten-free Worcestershire sauce**

1 tablespoon chopped **fresh chives** and **parsley**

1 **egg**, beaten

a handful of **sesame seeds**

mustard, to serve

salt and **freshly ground black pepper**

FOR THE PASTRY

200g **plain gluten-free flour**, plus extra for rolling

a pinch of **salt**

100g **lard**, cold and cut into chunks

1 teaspoon **modified tapioca starch** or **baking fix** (optional)

1 **egg**

1 **egg yolk**

1. Heat the oven to 200°C/400°F/gas mark 6.

2. To make the pastry, place the flour and salt in a food processor and add the chopped lard. Add baking fix, if using (this will just help make it a bit more stretchy). Pulse to rub the fat into the flour until it resembles breadcrumbs.

3. Tip out into a bowl. Beat together the egg and egg yolk and add to the flour. Bring together to a soft dough. Wrap in clingfilm and rest in the refrigerator for about 15 minutes.

4. Heat the oil in a pan and cook the onion with the chopped leek and celery for about 10 minutes, until soft. Add the garlic and cook for another minute. Tip into a bowl and allow to cool.

5. Add the sausage meat, apple, mustards, sauce and herbs. Season well and combine with a fork.

6. Roll out the pastry on a floured surface until approximately 2mm thick. This can be done in 2 batches to make 2 rough oblongs. Work as quickly as you can, as the pastry will tend to crack. You can always patch it up – this is not a disaster.

7. Place some of the sausage meat mixture in the centre of each pastry oblong and brush around the edge with the beaten egg. Fold over one half of each oblong and seal the edges. Trim and brush with egg wash, then sprinkle with sesame seeds. Cut your large sausage into smaller sausages.

8. Place on a baking tray lined with baking parchment and pop into the preheated oven for 15 minutes, then drop the heat down to 160°C/325°F/gas mark 3 and bake for another 10 minutes. Let cool and serve with mustard.

Try swapping the sausage meat for chorizo or black pudding (gluten- and dairy-free versions, of course). The pastry can also be used for a pie topping.

FAVA BEAN PURÉE WITH CHARD

A staple dish from Puglia, this is normally served with braised chicory
but chard makes a good substitute.

PREP TIME: 10 MINS · SOAK TIME: OVERNIGHT · COOK TIME: 45 MINS

200g **dried split** and peeled **fava beans**, soaked overnight in plenty of **cold water**

6 cloves of **garlic**, 4 peeled and left whole, 2 crushed

150ml **extra virgin olive oil**, plus extra for drizzling

200g **rainbow chard leaves**, stalks removed

a pinch of **red chilli flakes**

1 tablespoon **olive oil**

salt and **freshly ground black pepper**

1. Drain the beans and rinse well. Place in a large pan and cover with water. Add the whole cloves of garlic and bring to a simmer. Cook over a low heat, making sure the beans are always covered with water, for about 40 minutes, or until the beans are soft. Place in a colander or sieve and leave to drain over the sink for about 10 minutes.

2. Transfer the beans to a food processor with the whole cloves of garlic. Add one of the crushed garlic cloves, season well and blitz while adding the extra virgin olive oil until you have a smooth purée. You may need to add more oil – the purée should be smooth and creamy. It will thicken up as it cools down. Check the seasoning.

3. Chop the chard stalks and blanch in plenty of boiling salted water for a minute. Add the leaves and cook for 30 seconds. Drain, refresh and squeeze out any excess water. Cook the remaining crushed garlic clove and the chilli flakes for a minute in the olive oil. Toss the cooked chard with the flavoured oil and season well.

4. Serve the purée drizzled with a little oil and with the braised chard alongside.

70g **dried porcini mushrooms**

1 **onion** and 1 **leek**, finely chopped

2 tablespoons **olive oil**

250g **risotto rice**

1 clove of **garlic**, crushed

a splash of **vermouth** or **white wine**

400ml **vegetable stock** (optional)

a dash of **truffle oil**

fresh **parsley** and **chives**, chopped

cornflour, to coat

2 **eggs**, beaten

polenta, to coat

rapeseed oil, for deep frying

salt and **freshly ground black pepper**

PORCINI ARANCINI

Polenta makes a super substitution for traditional breadcrumbs. Thank you to Hannah Bould for lending us her awesome bowls (pictured right) and having the most career-appropriate name ever.

**PREP TIME: 15 MINS · SOAK TIME: 30 MINS
COOK TIME: 45 MINS**

1. Soak the mushrooms in 400ml of boiling water for at least 30 minutes.

2. Cook the onion and leek in the oil for about 15 minutes over a low heat without colouring. Drain the porcini, reserving the soaking liquid, and chop finely. Add the mushrooms to the vegetables along with the rice and garlic, then turn up the heat. Cook for 2 minutes, then season well and add the splash of booze.

3. Slowly add the porcini cooking liquid, stirring after each addition. Cook for about 20 minutes, adding some of the stock if you run out of liquid. When the rice is just cooked, remove from the heat and stir in the truffle oil and herbs. Season well and transfer to a tray or bowl. Allow to cool.

4. Shape the rice into balls the size of golf balls. Roll first in cornflour, then in beaten egg and finally in polenta. Heat the oil to 180°C and deep-fry the arancini for about 4 minutes, or until golden brown and hot in the middle. Serve sprinkled with extra salt.

150ml **almond milk**

7g sachet of **dried yeast**

100g **buckwheat flour**

50g **millet flour**

1 teaspoon **baking powder**

1 teaspoon **caraway seeds**, crushed

2 **eggs**, separated

rice bran oil, for frying

salt and **freshly ground black pepper**

BUCKWHEAT BLINIS

Once cooked, these will keep in the freezer for a few months for spontaneous hosting with the mosting.

**PREP TIME: 15 MINS · RISE TIME: 2 HOURS
COOK TIME: 15 MINS**

1. Warm the almond milk to tepid, whisk in the yeast and rest for 10 minutes.

2. Sift the flours and baking powder into a large bowl. Add the caraway seeds.

3. Whisk the egg yolks into the yeast mix and slowly add to the dry ingredients to make a thick batter. Cover and leave to rise for an hour.

4. Whisk the egg whites until just holding. Fold into the batter and leave for another hour. Season.

5. Heat a little oil in a non-stick frying pan. Drop spoonfuls of the batter into the pan and cook for 2 minutes on each side. Drain on kitchen paper before serving.

ASIAN PRAWN PANCAKES

This coconut pancake recipe is from *Everyday and Sunday: Recipes from Riverford Farm*, which Jane wrote a while ago.

PREP TIME: 15 MINS · COOK TIME: 25 MINS

FOR THE PANCAKES

150g **rice flour**

50g **gram flour**

1 large **egg**, beaten

90g **creamed coconut**, grated and mixed with 300ml **boiling water**

1 teaspoon **salt**

1 teaspoon **ground turmeric**

1 teaspoon **coconut sugar**

juice of 2 **limes**

2 tablespoons **rice bran oil**

FOR THE FILLING

250g **raw prawns**

90g **desiccated coconut**, covered in **boiling water** for 30 minutes, then excess water squeezed out

1 tablespoon chopped **fresh coriander**

2 cloves of **garlic**, crushed

2 **red chillies**, chopped

8 tablespoons **rice bran oil**

2 teaspoons **fish sauce**

1 tablespoon **coconut sugar**

1 teaspoon **salt**

1 teaspoon **freshly ground black pepper**

1 ripe **mango**, finely diced

1. Sieve the flours together and mix with an egg in a food processor, gradually adding the creamed coconut followed by the rest of the pancake ingredients except for the oil. The batter should have the consistency of single cream. Allow to rest for 1 hour.

2. For the filling, grind the prawns and coconut together in a food processor.

3. Make a paste with the coriander, garlic and chillies by pounding them together in a pestle and mortar. Cook the paste in the rice bran oil for 2 minutes. Add the prawns and coconut and continue cooking for 10 minutes, until the prawns are cooked. Season with the rest of the ingredients, then add the diced mango.

4. In a non-stick pan, heat the oil and cook the pancakes in batches by dropping in a dessertspoon at a time, and spreading them out with the back of a spoon – they should have a yellow lacy appearance. Turn over after 2 minutes to cook the other side.

5. Remove from the pan and top with a little of the mango filling to serve.

Leaves from a few sprigs of basil, mint and coriander can be mixed with beansprouts and served with these pancakes.

FISH SOUP

This is based on the recipe for fish soup in *The Carved Angel Cookery Book* by Joyce Molyneux. The soup is thickened by whisking in aïoli and gently cooking. For something a bit more substantial, add chunks of firm white fish and poach in the soup.

PREP TIME: 20 MINS · COOK TIME: 50 MINS

3 tablespoons **olive oil**

1 **onion**, chopped

½ **head of fennel**, chopped

½ **leek**, chopped

½ **cucumber**, chopped

1 stick of **celery**, chopped

a pinch of **saffron**

3 sprigs of **thyme**

4 cloves of **garlic**, crushed

1 × 400g tin of **chopped tomatoes**

1 tablespoon chopped **fresh chives**

1 tablespoon chopped **fresh dill**

1 tablespoon chopped **fresh basil**

200ml **white wine**

450ml **fish stock**

100g **smoked haddock**

juice of ½ **lemon**

salt and **freshly ground black pepper**

2 tablespoons chopped **fresh parsley**, to garnish

FOR THE AÏOLI

1 large **egg yolk** (room temperature)

2 cloves of **garlic**, crushed

150ml **olive oil**

lemon juice, to taste

salt and **freshly ground black pepper**

1. Heat the oil in a large pan. Quickly blitz the vegetables in batches in a food processor so they are chopped very small but not mushy. Add to the pan along with the saffron and thyme. Cook for 20 minutes over a low heat.

2. Add the garlic and cook for a minute. Blitz the tomatoes with the herbs and add to the veg. Simmer for 10 minutes, until the tomatoes have reduced. Add the wine and simmer for 5 minutes, then add the fish stock. Cover and simmer for another 10 minutes, then add the fish and leave to poach in the stock for a further 5 minutes. Season well.

3. In a large bowl, whisk the egg yolk with the garlic and slowly start to add the olive oil, whisking continuously. Add the oil in a steady stream until you have a thick emulsion. Season and add lemon juice to taste.

4. To serve, whisk the aïoli into the soup and heat gently, whisking until the soup thickens. Serve with a sprinkling of parsley.

We've stirred through a dollop of the red pepper sauce from page 54 here too.

FRIED DUMPLINGS

You can substitute minced prawns, pork or mushrooms for the chicken. Instead of regular dumpling wrappers, these bean curd/tofu skins are wonderfully gluten-free.

PREP TIME: 20 MINS · COOK TIME: 10 MINS

1 × 50g pack **bean curd/tofu skins**
rice bran oil, for shallow-frying

FOR THE FILLING
300g **chicken breast**
100g **mushrooms**
4 **spring onions**, chopped
1 tablespoon chopped **fresh chives**
1 teaspoon **tamari**
1 teaspoon **sesame oil**
1 teaspoon **rice wine**
a pinch of **five-spice powder**
a pinch of **ground white pepper**
a thumb-sized piece of **ginger**, grated
1 teaspoon **chilli paste**
½ **egg white**, whisked with 1 teaspoon **arrowroot**

1. Finely chop the chicken and mushrooms. Mix with the other ingredients, except for the tofu skins and oil for frying.

2. Separate the bean curd skins. Before using, soak each one in a little warm water to make it pliable – this should be no longer than 5–10 seconds, or the skin will begin to cook. Place a skin on a clean cloth (this helps it to not stick to your chopping board) and spread a tablespoon of prawn mix at one end of the oblong. Fold in the sides and roll up the skin tightly to make a long spring roll shape. Repeat until all the filling is used.

3. Heat about 2cm of oil in a pan and fry the rolls, with the join underneath to prevent them splitting, in batches, until lightly browned and crisp.

4. Serve with a dipping sauce (see tip below).

Our favourite dipping sauce for these type of dumplings uses chiankiang vinegar, a mild and dark Chinese black vinegar. Mix 3–4 tablespoons of chiankiang vinegar with some grated fresh ginger and a thinly sliced clove of garlic. If you can't source the vinegar, a tamari and rice vinegar mixture will be great too.

TOP DIPS

Double-dipping is highly recommended. We served these with a bunch of crudité vegetables. Use whatever is in season, and serve them on a bed of crushed ice to keep them pretty and perky.

CAULIFLOWER & ANCHOVY PURÉE

PREP TIME: 5 MINS · COOK TIME: 15 MINS

1 tablespoon **olive oil**

1 **cauliflower**, cut into florets

2 cloves of **garlic**, crushed

3 **anchovies**

vegetable stock

freshly ground black pepper

1. Heat the oil in a large pan and add the cauliflower florets, garlic and anchovies. Stir, season and cover. Turn the heat down to very low and allow the cauliflower to steam and braise until tender.

2. Transfer to a blender, making sure all the bits of garlic and anchovy are scraped out of the pan. Pour in vegetable stock until you have a smooth purée, and season with the pepper.

FENNEL & ROSEMARY DIP

PREP TIME: 10 MINS · COOK TIME: 50 MINS

3 heads of **fennel**

2 tablespoon **olive oil**

1 clove of **garlic**, crushed

2 teaspoons chopped **fresh rosemary**

juice of ½ **lemon**

salt and **freshly ground black pepper**

1. Trim the fennel and cut into thin wedges. Heat the oil in a large pan, add the fennel, and cook over a high heat for 5 minutes, until the wedges are lightly browned.

2. Move the fennel to one side of the pan and add the garlic and rosemary. Cook for a minute, then stir into the fennel. Season well, cover and turn down the heat. Cook for about 30 minutes, adding water if the fennel starts to catch on the pan.

3. When the fennel is cooked through, add the lemon juice to the mixture and purée in a blender, adding a little water if needed. Season well.

500g **beetroot**

50ml **olive oil**, plus 1 teaspoon

50ml **water**

1 × 1cm piece of **ginger**, grated

2 tablespoons chopped **fresh mint**

½ teaspoon **ground cumin**

½ clove of **garlic**, crushed

1 **avocado**

salt and **freshly ground black pepper**

SPICED BEETROOT

PREP TIME: 10 MINS · COOK TIME: 50 MINS

1. Heat the oven to 170°C/350°F/gas mark 3.

2. Clean the beetroot and toss in a teaspoon of olive oil. Place in an ovenproof tray with the water, season and cover tightly. Bake for about 50 minutes, or until tender.

3. When cool enough to handle, trim and remove the skin. Cut the beetroot into small chunks. Purée in a blender with the rest of the olive oil and all the other ingredients, until smooth.

3

EVERYDAY EASY

GRILLED CAULIFLOWER STEAKS WITH ROMESCO

Miss steak? Surely some mistake. These won't make you feel like you are in Texas. They are even better than that.

PREP TIME: 20 MINS · COOK TIME: 45 MINS

1 large **cauliflower**

1 teaspoon **olive oil**

12 **spring onions**

parsley leaves

FOR THE ROMESCO SAUCE

3 **tomatoes**

8 cloves of **garlic**, unpeeled

100ml **extra virgin olive oil**

50g **flaked almonds**

50g **hazelnuts**, peeled

200g **piquillo peppers**

2 **red chillies**

1 teaspoon **paprika**

50ml **sherry vinegar**

salt and **freshly ground black pepper**

1. Heat the oven to 180°C/350°F/gas mark 4.

2. Roast the tomatoes and garlic with 1 teaspoon of the oil on a baking tray in the oven for 20 minutes. When cool enough to touch, peel the garlic and tomatoes and place the flesh in a food processor.

3. Roast the nuts in the oven for 10 minutes, until lightly browned. Allow to cool.

4. Add the nuts to the processor along with the peppers, chillies and paprika. Blitz, slowly adding the rest of the oil and vinegar. Check the seasoning.

5. Place the cauliflower on a chopping board stem side up and cut down through the core so you have 4 steaks about 1–2cm thick. Any excess cauliflower can be used for another dish or for cauli-rice. Brush with olive oil and season well.

6. Trim the spring onions. Heat a griddle plate or pan until very hot. Place the spring onions on the plate and grill for a minute on either side. Remove to a plate, then cook the cauliflower steaks for 3 minutes on either side until lightly charred and tender. A contact grill can be also be used.

7. Arrange the cauliflower steaks and spring onions on a serving dish and drizzle with the romesco sauce. Serve sprinkled with parsley leaves.

FAVOURITE FAVA FALAFEL

These are a type of Egyptian falafel, and we sphinx they rock (work with us). Made with fava beans (broadly speaking, like broad beans), they are light, moist and utterly delightful. You can by dried split fava beans online or in Asian or Middle Eastern supermarkets.

PREP TIME: 20 MINS · COOK TIME: 10 MINS
SOAK TIME: OVERNIGHT

3 tablespoons **sesame seeds**

rapeseed, **rice bran** or **sunflower oil**, for frying

FOR THE FALAFEL

250g **dried split fava beans** (soaked in lots of **cold water** overnight)

1 clove of **garlic**, crushed

1 **leek**, finely chopped

5 **spring onions**, chopped

½ teaspoon **bicarbonate of soda**

2 teaspoons **gram flour**

1 tablespoon chopped **fresh coriander**

1 tablespoon chopped **fresh parsley**

1 teaspoon **ground cumin**

a pinch of **cayenne pepper**

salt and **freshly ground black pepper**

FOR THE MINTY TAHINI SAUCE

3 tablespoons **tahini**

½ clove of **garlic**, crushed

50ml **olive oil**

juice of ½ **lemon**

a pinch of **cayenne pepper**

salt and **freshly ground black pepper**

2 tablespoons chopped **fresh mint**

1. Drain the split fava beans well in a sieve or colander. Tip into a food processor along with the rest of the falafel ingredients. Grind to a rough paste, and tip out on to a clean surface.

2. Divide the mix into balls about the size of a small golf ball. The mix should make 12–16 balls. Press them down with your fingers to make small patties.

3. Sprinkle a few tablespoons of sesame seeds on a plate and coat each side of the falafels roughly with the seeds. Allow them to sit in the refrigerator for at least 10 minutes.

4. To cook the falafel, heat the oil in a small pan to the depth of a few centimetres. The oil will be ready when a piece of bread dropped in sizzles and turns brown quickly. Turn the heat down and start to cook the falafel in batches. We cook them 4 at a time and keep them warm on a baking tray in a low oven. Cook each side for 2–3 minutes, or until they are golden brown, then flip them over and fry the other side.

5. Whisk all the ingredients for the minty tahini sauce together and let down to pouring consistency with a little cold water. Serve.

Don't over-blitz the mixture, it'll be harder to roll neatly.

NASI GORENG

This is an Indonesian staple, and it's perfect for using up leftovers. Pork, chicken, vegetables – they're all welcome in this mish-mash.

PREP TIME: 15 MINS · SOAK TIME: OVERNIGHT

1 large head of **cauliflower**

4 **eggs**, beaten

1 tablespoon **rice bran oil**

2 tablespoons **dried prawns**

4 cloves of **garlic**, crushed

2 **red chillies**, chopped

1 tablespoon **roasted peanuts**

1 × 2cm piece of **ginger**, grated

2 tablespoons **coconut oil**

2 **shallots**, chopped

2 **chicken breasts**, thinly sliced

200g **raw prawns**

1 tablespoon **kejap manis**

1 bunch of **spring onions**, chopped

salt and **freshly ground black pepper**

TO SERVE

coriander leaves

½ **cucumber**, sliced

16 **cherry tomatoes**, halved

fried **eggs** (optional)

1. Cut off the florets from the cauliflower and blitz in a food processor until you have very small pieces, like rice.

2. Beat the eggs and season well. Heat the rice bran oil in a large non-stick pan. Pour in a little of the egg mix and tip the pan so you have a thin omelette. Cook for a minute, then tip out of the pan on to a tray. Repeat until all the egg mix is used up. Roll up the omelettes and slice into 1cm pieces.

3. Cover the dried prawns with boiling water and set aside. Mix together the garlic, chillies, peanuts and ginger in a pestle and mortar (or a blender) and pound to a thick paste. Drain the prawns, reserving the soaking water, and chop finely. Add to the paste.

4. Heat the coconut oil in a large pan and fry the paste for a minute without browning. Add the shallots and sliced chicken breast and stir-fry for about 5 minutes, stirring continuously. Tip in the raw prawns and cook for a further 2 minutes. The prawns and chicken should be firm to touch.

5. Add the cauliflower and cook over a medium heat for 5 minutes, stirring well to combine, adding a little of the reserved prawn soaking water if the rice starts to stick to the pan.

6. Stir in the kejap manis, sliced omelette and spring onions. Check the seasoning and serve with coriander leaves and with cucumber and tomatoes sliced on the side.

7. The nasi goreng can be topped with a fried egg to serve, if you fancy it.

AUBERGINE POLPETTINI

Itsy bitsy teeny weeny aubergine-y polpettini. These little meatless balls are a speciality in Puglia – they can be served fried as a snack with drinks, or as below with a tomato sauce. Leave out the chilli and they're much more teeny people friendly (kids).

PREP TIME: 25 MINS · COOK TIME: 1 HOUR

2 large **aubergines**, peeled

1 tablespoon **olive oil**, plus extra for frying

1 tablespoon **capers**, soaked and drained

2 tablespoons chopped **fresh basil**

1 tablespoon chopped **fresh mint**

1 tablespoon chopped **fresh parsley**

a large pinch of **wild oregano**

1 clove of **garlic**, crushed

1 **egg**, beaten

50g **ground almonds**

50g **almond flour**

3 tablespoons **fine cornmeal**

salt and **freshly ground black pepper**

TOMATO SAUCE

2 **onions**, finely chopped

10 cloves of **garlic**, crushed

2 **red chillies**, chopped (optional)

2 × 400g tins of **chopped tomatoes**

TO SERVE

fresh basil leaves, ripped, to serve

10 **black olives**, stoned and roughly chopped

1. Slice the aubergines into ½cm slices, then cut each slice into small dice. Heat the tablespoon of oil in a large pan. Tip in the diced aubergine and stir. Fry for a minute, season and cover. Cook over a low heat for 5 minutes, or until tender, then place in a sieve and press out any excess moisture.

2. Put the aubergine into a large bowl and add the capers, herbs, garlic, egg and ground almonds. Mix well and season. Place half the mix in a food processor and pulse for 10 seconds, then spoon back into the bowl and mix with the remaining unprocessed aubergine.

3. Shape into small balls, about the size of a large walnut, and roll first in the almond flour and then in the cornmeal. Heat some oil in a large non-stick frying pan and gently fry the balls for about 5 minutes, until browned all over. Remove from the pan and tip out any excess oil.

4. To make the Tomato Sauce add the onions to the pan and cook over a gentle heat for 10 minutes. Add the garlic and chopped chillies, cook for another 2 minutes, then tip in the chopped tomatoes. Stir well and bring up to a simmer, then cook gently for about 30 minutes. Return the polpette to the pan and cook gently for 5 minutes.

5. Serve sprinkled with the torn basil leaves and chopped olives.

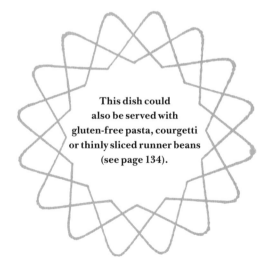

This dish could also be served with gluten-free pasta, courgetti or thinly sliced runner beans (see page 134).

225g **split mung beans**

50g **glutinous rice**

1 tablespoon **tamari**

1 tablespoon **toasted sesame oil**

½ teaspoon **bicarbonate of soda**

100g **beansprouts**

1 clove of **garlic**, crushed

100g **pork mince**, cooked

1 bunch of **spring onions**,
   chopped

100g **kimchi**, drained and
   chopped (optional)

oil, for frying

FOR THE DIPPING SAUCE

2 tablespoons **tamari**

1 tablespoon **rice vinegar**

2 teaspoons **raw honey**

100g **gluten-free plain flour**

2 teaspoons **baking powder**

100ml **dashi** or **fish stock**

2 **eggs**, beaten

100g **smoked salmon**, thinly sliced

200g **white cabbage**, shredded

½ **kohlrabi**, grated

1 bunch of **spring onions**, finely
   chopped

rice bran oil

mayonnaise

130g **okonomiyaki sauce**

salt and **cayenne pepper**

OPTIONAL TOPPINGS

**pickled ginger, bonito fish flakes,
nori**, chopped **fresh chives, sesame
seeds**

BINDAEDUK

When we started LEON, we always used mung beans as an example of things that you would think of negatively as being a little too worthy ('It's a bit mung beans and open-toe sandals'). These savoury Korean pancakes require no sacrifice. They are as lovely as they are good for you.

PREP TIME: 10 MINS · SOAK TIME: OVERNIGHT
COOK TIME: 25 MINS

1. Soak the mung beans and rice in plenty of cold water for at least 8 hours. Drain, then blend with extra water to the consistency of double cream.

2. Mix together the dipping sauce ingredients with 1 tablespoon of water and 1 of the chopped spring onions and set aside.

3. Stir the rest of the ingredients, except for the oil, into the mung bean batter. Heat 2 tablespoons of oil in a non-stick frying pan and fry a quarter of the mix in as a round pancake, pressing down a little. Fry for 3 minutes on each side, until golden brown. Repeat until all the mix is used up.

4. Serve with the dipping sauce.

OKONOMIYAKI

These Japanese pancakes can be topped with lots of different sauces – they literally mean 'what you like'. You'll like them. Promise.

PREP TIME: 15 MINS · COOK TIME: 10 MINS

1. Sift the flour into a large bowl with the baking powder. Add the stock and the eggs and whisk together to combine. Fold in the salmon and vegetables.

2. Heat a little oil in a large non-stick frying pan and pour in the batter to make a shape about 1.5cm thick. You can make smaller pancakes, or one or two large ones. Cook for 4 minutes on each side, or until the pancakes are firm to touch.

3. Remove from the pan and drizzle with the mayo and okonomiyaki sauce. (If you can't find okonomiyaki sauce then mix together 90g tomato sauce, 30g Worcestershire sauce and 10g tamari – check the ingredients lists first though.)

4. Top with any of the suggested ingredients. If you have made one large pancake, slice it up to serve.

CASHEW COURGETTI
WITH CHICKEN

This basic cashew sauce makes a great béchamel replacement – it has an incredibly creamy and cheesy taste. Pick small courgettes as they'll be the least waterlogged and won't dilute your sauce. We actually think the American term for courgetti, 'zoodles', is far more fun. Toodles, zoodles.

PREP TIME: 15 MINS · SOAK TIME: OVERNIGHT · COOK TIME: 10 MINS

100g **cashew nuts**, soaked overnight in lots of **cold water**

250ml **strong chicken stock**

2 cloves of **garlic**, crushed

3 tablespoons **olive oil**

zest and juice of 1 **lemon**

150g **peas**

100g **cooked chicken**, shredded

leaves from 1 bunch of **fresh basil**, shredded

750g **courgettes**, spiralized or cut into long thin strips

salt and **freshly ground black pepper**

1. Heat the oven to 220°C/425°F/gas mark 7.

2. Drain the cashew nuts and blend with the chicken stock until smooth.

3. Cook the garlic in a little olive oil and add the cashew sauce. Stir well to combine and bring up to a simmer. Turn the heat down and add the lemon zest and juice, peas, chicken and basil. Season well.

4. Toss the courgette strips in the rest of the olive oil and season. Place on a baking tray lined with baking paper and put into the oven for 5 minutes. Remove and toss with the sauce to serve.

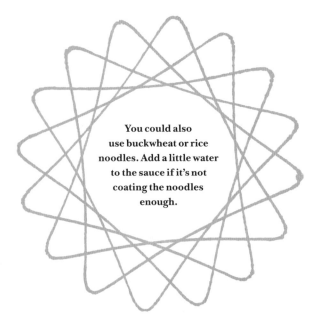

You could also use buckwheat or rice noodles. Add a little water to the sauce if it's not coating the noodles enough.

BUCKWHEAT
BEETROOT SALAD

This earthy, sweet and savoury salad will leave you singing Bohemian Radishy.
Dry-toasting buckwheat adds an interesting texture and nutty flavour for salads.

PREP TIME: 15 MINS · COOK TIME: 5 MINS

200g **buckwheat**

2 tablespoons **caraway seeds**

200g **beetroot**, peeled and grated

2 small **carrots**, peeled and grated

juice of 1 **orange**

2 tablespoons **olive oil**

2 teaspoons **pomegranate
    molasses**

½ head of **radicchio**, shredded

seeds from 1 **pomegranate**

4 **radishes**, sliced

1 tablespoon chopped **fresh dill**

salt and **freshly ground black
    pepper**

1. Heat a non-stick frying pan and dry-roast the buckwheat with the caraway seeds until golden and fragrant. Remove from the heat and allow to cool.

2. Toss with the grated beetroot and carrot. Mix together the orange juice, olive oil and pomegranate molasses and season. Drizzle half over the beetroot and toss together.

3. Arrange the shredded radicchio on a serving dish. Top with the beetroot and buckwheat. Sprinkle with pomegranate seeds and radish slices. Finish with chopped dill to serve.

50g **pecans**

2 teaspoons **olive oil**

a pinch of **cayenne pepper**

a pinch of **smoked paprika**

1 bunch of **cavolo nero**, leaves
   removed from central rib

1 head of **chicory**, sliced

1 **apple**, thinly sliced

1 tablespoon **lemon juice**

1 **red chilli**, chopped

1 **avocado**, chopped

salt

FOR THE DRESSING

3 tablespoons chopped **fresh dill**

1 tablespoon **maple syrup**

1 tablespoon **Muscatel** (or
   white wine) **vinegar**

3 tablespoons **extra virgin olive oil**

KALE, AVOCADO
& APPLE SALAD

A salad that is dressed to kale. If you're looking for an extra protein fix,
some pan-seared salmon would work on the side, or flaked through.

PREP TIME: 10 MINS · COOK TIME: 6 MINS

1. Heat the oven to 180°C/350°F/gas mark 4.

2. Toss the nuts with a little olive oil, cayenne, salt and smoked paprika. Place
on a baking tray and put into the oven for about 6 minutes, or until the nuts
are lightly toasted. Allow to cool, then chop roughly.

3. Shred the cavolo nero and place in a bowl with the rest of the salad
ingredients. Whisk together the dressing ingredients and toss with the salad.
Sprinkle with the chopped pecans to serve.

EVERYDAY EASY

NUTTY SWEDES

1 **swede**, about 400g, peeled

1 **apple**

2 **dried pears**, thinly sliced

50g **hazelnuts**, toasted (skins off) and crushed

1 tablespoon **cider vinegar**

2 teaspoons **wholegrain mustard**

2 tablespoons **hazelnut oil**

1 tablespoon **rice malt syrup**

2 tablespoons chopped **fresh parsley**

salt and **freshly ground black pepper**

How swede it is to be loved by you. Swedes should not be confined to neeps and tatties. Raw swedes give a slightly sweet, slightly mustardy flavour to this wintry salad.

PREP TIME: 10 MINS

1. Grate the peeled swede into fine julienne. Peel the apple, chop the flesh into small dice, and mix with the swede in a large bowl. Add the sliced dried pear and the nuts.

2. Mix together the vinegar, mustard, oil and syrup and whisk to combine. Toss with the swede and season well. Sprinkle with chopped parsley to serve.

STEAK, SOBA & SHIITAKE

Perfectly cooked steak and mushrooms. Soba hot right now.

PREP TIME: 20 MINS · MARINATE TIME: 1 HOUR · COOK TIME: 15 MINS

400g **sirloin steak** (or **rump**)

1 clove of **garlic**, crushed

1 teaspoon **coconut sugar**

2 tablespoons **tamari**

1 tablespoon **rice vinegar**

2 teaspoons **freshly ground black pepper**

200g **soba noodles**

1 tablespoon **sesame oil**

2 tablespoons **rice bran oil**

3 cloves of **garlic**, crushed

a pinch of **ground Sichuan pepper**

150g **shiitake mushrooms**, roughly sliced

100g **chestnut mushrooms**, roughly sliced

3 tablespoons **rice wine**

3 tablespoons **mirin**

1 tablespoon **tamari**

150g **asparagus spears**, cut into 2–3cm lengths

TO SERVE

watercress

6 **spring onions**, chopped

coriander leaves

1. Trim the steak into 2cm chunks. Mix the next 5 ingredients together and marinate the meat in this for at least an hour.

2. Cook the soba noodles in plenty of boiling salted water for 5 minutes (or as per the instructions on the packet). Drain and toss in the sesame oil.

3. Heat a tablespoon of oil in a large pan and add the garlic and Sichuan pepper. Cook for a minute, then add the mushrooms. Cook over a high heat for 2 minutes, then add the wine, mirin, tamari and asparagus. Bring to a simmer and cook for 2 minutes. Fold in the soba noodles.

4. Heat the remaining tablespoon of oil until very hot in a non-stick frying pan and cook the steak pieces in batches for a minute, being very careful not to overcook them. They just need to be sealed on all sides – shaking the pan will help you do this (and make you look very cheffy).

5. Place the noodles and watercress on a serving dish. Top with the beef and serve sprinkled with spring onions and coriander leaves.

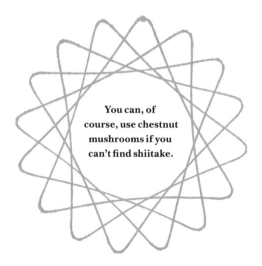

You can, of course, use chestnut mushrooms if you can't find shiitake.

SWEET STUFF

The way the corn is cooked for these stuffed sweet potatoes is great on its own too.

PREP TIME: 20 MINS · COOK TIME: 40 MINS

4 **sweet potatoes**

2 tablespoons **olive oil**

6 rashers of **streaky bacon**, chopped

1 **red onion**, chopped

1 teaspoon **fresh thyme leaves**

½ teaspoon **ground cumin**

kernels from 2 **cobs of corn**

1 **red pepper**, diced

2 **red chillies**, chopped

1 clove of **garlic**, crushed

50ml **white wine**

TO SERVE

1 **avocado**, chopped

juice of 1 **lime**

1 tablespoon chopped **fresh coriander**

2 tablespoons **mayonnaise**

1 teaspoon **chipotle paste**

1. Heat the oven to 190°C/375°F/gas mark 5.

2. Place the sweet potatoes directly on the rack of the oven and bake for approximately 40 minutes, or until tender.

3. While the potatoes are cooking, heat the oil in a large pan and cook the bacon for 5 minutes. Add the onion, thyme, cumin and corn. Cook over a high heat for 5 minutes to lightly brown the corn, stirring well.

4. Add the red pepper, chillies and garlic. Cook for a minute, then add the wine. Stir well and cook for another 10 minutes. If the ingredients start to catch on the bottom of the pan, add a little water.

5. Mix the chopped avocado with lime juice and coriander. Blend the mayonnaise with the chipotle paste.

6. Remove the sweet potatoes from the oven. Cut in half lengthways and fluff up the flesh with a fork. Spoon some of the corn mix on to each potato, scatter with the avocado and drizzle with the chipotle mayonnaise (make sure there's no added sugar) to serve.

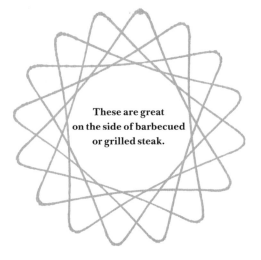

These are great
on the side of barbecued
or grilled steak.

TEMPEH & MUSHROOM LARB

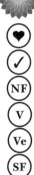

Minced meat larb is the national dish of Laos. Here, we've made mushrooms the star of the show, with the added bonus of fermented tempeh, which is great for your health. If you're vegetarian or vegan, having to exclude recipes because of fish sauce is mightily annoying. This alternative makes 100ml but keeps well in a sealed container. Nothing fishy about that.

PREP TIME: 15 MINS · COOK TIME: 10 MINS

2 tablespoons **jasmine rice**

1 tablespoon **rice bran oil**

2 **green chillies**, chopped

1 tablespoon **lemongrass**, chopped

200g **tempeh**, broken into 1–2cm pieces

200g **shiitake mushrooms**, chopped into wedges

100g **button mushrooms**, chopped into wedges

2 tablespoons chopped **fresh coriander**

3 tablespoons chopped **fresh mint**

1 **red onion**, finely chopped

2 **Little Gem lettuces**, shredded

½ **cucumber**, cut into batons

¼ **mooli**, shredded

a pinch of **cayenne pepper**

FOR VEGAN FISH SAUCE

170g **shredded seaweed**

3 cloves of **garlic**, whole

1 teaspoon **black peppercorns**

100ml **tamari**

½ tablespoon **miso**

FOR THE DRESSING

2 tablespoons **lime juice**

2 tablespoons **vegan fish sauce** (see above)

2 teaspoons **palm sugar**

1. Place the rice in a frying pan and toast over a medium heat until golden brown. Allow to cool and grind to a rough powder in a pestle and mortar or spice grinder.

2. Heat the oil in a large pan and cook the chillies and lemongrass for 2 minutes. Add the tempeh and mushrooms. Stir-fry for 5 minutes, then tip into a bowl. Allow to cool a little, then stir in the chopped herbs and red onion.

3. To make the vegan fish sauce, bring the seaweed, garlic and peppercorns to the boil with 700ml of water. Lower the heat and simmer for 20 minutes. Strain and return it to the pot with the tamari and cook until reduced and very salty. Remove from the heat and stir in the miso.

4. Arrange the lettuce, cucumber and mooli on a serving dish. Top with the mushroom mix. To make the dressing mix together the lime, 2 tablespoons vegan fish sauce and sugar and drizzle over the salad. Serve sprinkled with cayenne pepper and ground rice.

A squeeze of lime juice would be nice too.

CAULIFLOWER & TEMPEH SAMBAL

Sambal is an Indonesian chilli sauce, it's truly explosive.

PREP TIME: 15 MINS · COOK TIME: 20 MINS

1 tablespoon **rice bran oil**

3 cloves of **garlic**, crushed

1 **onion**, chopped

200g **tempeh**, cut into thin slices

florets of 1 small **cauliflower**

100g **edamame beans**

2 **tomatoes**, skinned and chopped

1 teaspoon **tamarind paste**

1 teaspoon **palm sugar**

salt and **freshly ground black pepper**

FOR THE CHILLI PASTE

4 **dried** and 4 **fresh red chillies**

1 **red onion**, chopped

1 tablespoon **capers**

2 **tomatoes**, skinned and chopped

1. Blend together the chilli paste ingredients in a food processor.

2. Heat the oil in a large frying pan or wok and cook the garlic and onion for a minute. Tip in the chilli paste and bring up to a simmer. Cook for about 10 minutes and season well.

3. Add the tempeh, vegetables, tomatoes and 100ml water, turn up the heat and stir-fry for a few minutes, making sure the sauce doesn't catch. Cover and cook over a gentle heat for 5 minutes, or until the cauliflower is just cooked.

4. Stir in the tamarind paste and palm sugar. Taste and adjust the seasoning before serving.

EVERYDAY EASY

½ small **cauliflower**, florets
  removed

3 tablespoons **olive oil**

1 **beefsteak tomato**

leaves from 2 bunches of **fresh
  flat-leaf parsley**

1 bunch of **fresh mint**, leaves
  removed

1 bunch of **spring onions**

lemon juice, to taste

a pinch of **sumac**

salt and **freshly ground black
  pepper**

CAULIFLOWER TABBOULEH

Tabbouleh shan't be taboo for the gluten-free crowd.

PREP TIME: 10 MINS · COOK TIME: 3 MINS

1. Blitz the cauliflower florets in a food processor until they resemble couscous. Heat 1 tablespoon of oil in a large shallow pan. Tip in the cauliflower and stir-fry for a few minutes, until lightly toasted. Season well and allow to cool.

2. Skin and deseed the tomato. Dice the tomato flesh finely. Chop the herbs and spring onions.

3. Mix the tomato, herbs and spring onions with the cauliflower. Stir in the rest of the olive oil and add lemon juice to taste. Serve sprinkled with a pinch of sumac.

THAI FRIED EGG SALAD

Thai the knot with this quick, punchy salad.

PREP TIME: 10 MINS · COOK TIME: 8 MINS

rapeseed oil, for frying

4 **eggs**

50g **pea shoots**

½ **red onion**, sliced

8 **cherry tomatoes**, quartered

1 **celery heart**, thinly sliced

a handful of **beansprouts**

FOR THE DRESSING

1 clove of **garlic**, crushed

2 tablespoons **fresh coriander stalks** and **leaves**, finely chopped

2 tablespoons **lime juice**

1 **red chilli**, chopped

2 teaspoons **vegan fish sauce** (see page 102)

2 teaspoons **palm sugar**

1. Heat about 2cm of oil in a wok until hot. Break the eggs into ramekins and carefully tip into the oil. The eggs should puff, crackle and crisp up. Cook for a minute on one side. Tip over for a few seconds, then remove from the oil with a slotted spoon on to kitchen paper. The eggs can be cooked 1 or 2 at a time.

2. Whisk together the dressing ingredients. Place the pea shoots, onion, tomatoes, celery and beansprouts in a bowl. Cut the cooked eggs into sixths and fold into the salad. Toss with the dressing and serve.

MISO HAPPY

The first time Jane made this marinated miso tofu salad, she left the cooked tofu out in the kitchen at the same time her son came home from school. It disappeared. Funny that.

PREP TIME: 20 MINS · SOAK TIME: 30 MINS · STAND TIME: 15 MINS
COOK TIME: 20 MINS

10g **sea spaghetti** (seaweed)

250g **very firm tofu**

1 tablespoon **olive oil**

1 tablespoon **tamari**

1 tablespoon **arrowroot** or **cornflour**

1 tablespoon **sesame seeds**

100g **edamame beans**, cooked

50g **baby spinach**

¼ **cucumber**, peeled and shaved into strips

1 bunch of **spring onions**, thinly sliced

6 **radishes**, thinly sliced

1 tablespoon **black sesame seeds**

FOR THE MISO WASABI SAUCE

2 teaspoons **miso paste**

1 teaspoon **wasabi paste** (or more if desired)

1 tablespoon **rice wine vinegar**

1 teaspoon **ketjap manis**

1 tablespoon **grapeseed oil**

1 teaspoon **toasted sesame oil**

1. Heat the oven to 200°C/400°F/gas mark 6.

2. Soak the sea spaghetti in lots of boiling water for at least 30 minutes. Drain and rinse well.

3. Press the block of tofu and dry with kitchen paper. Cut into 1–2cm squares. In a bowl, mix together the olive oil and tamari. Toss the tofu through the mix and leave for 15 minutes.

4. Sieve the arrowroot or cornflour over the tofu and fold through with the sesame seeds. Place on a baking tray lined with baking parchment and put into the oven for about 20 minutes, until golden brown. Give the tray a shake halfway through the cooking time.

5. While the tofu is in the oven mix together the sauce ingredients in a bowl. Remove the tofu from the oven and allow to cool for 10 minutes. Add to the sauce and fold through to combine.

6. In a large bowl, toss the tofu and its marinade with the drained sea spaghetti and edamame beans. Arrange the spinach and cucumber on a serving dish and top with the tofu, beans and seaweed. Sprinkle with the spring onions, radishes and black sesame seeds to serve.

VEGETABLE HARIRA

When people ask you how you made such a fiercely flavourful soup, tell them it's a souprise. (Sorry.) A lot of chopping goes into this soup, but if you have a food processor, let it do all the work for you. All the vegetables can be swapped in this recipe, just use whatever you have.

PREP TIME: 20 MINS · COOK TIME: 50 MINS
SOAK TIME: OVERNIGHT

200g **yellow split peas**, soaked overnight in **cold water**

2 tablespoons **olive oil**

1 **onion**, finely chopped

a pinch of **saffron**

1 × 2cm stick of **cinnamon**

2 **carrots**, finely chopped

2 sticks of **celery**, finely chopped

1 **leek**, finely chopped

4 **turnips**, cut into 1–2cm chunks

2 **parsnips**, cut into 1–2cm chunks

200g **swede**, cut into 1–2cm chunks

3 cloves of **garlic**, crushed

½ teaspoon **ground turmeric**

1 teaspoon **ground coriander**

1 × 400g tin of **chopped tomatoes**

1 litre **vegetable stock**

1 × 400g tin of **chickpeas**, drained

100g **spinach**

1 tablespoon chopped **fresh mint**

1 tablespoon chopped **fresh coriander**

salt and **freshly ground black pepper**

1. Drain the yellow split peas and place in a pan. Cover with water and bring to the boil, then turn down the heat and simmer for 20–30 minutes, while you get started cooking the vegetables.

2. Heat the oil in a large pan and add the onion, saffron, cinnamon, carrots, celery and leek. Cook for about 15 minutes over a low heat, without browning.

3. Add the turnips, parsnips and swede to the pan with the garlic and spices. Drain the split peas and add them to the vegetables along with the tinned tomatoes and stock. Bring to the boil, then reduce the heat and simmer for 30 minutes, or until the split peas are tender. Scoop out a couple of ladlefuls and blend until smooth, either with a stick blender or in a food processor. Return this to the pan and stir into the rest of the soup.

4. Add the chickpeas and spinach and stir into the soup. Cook for another 5 minutes, adding water to thin down if necessary, then season.

5. Add a little more stock if the soup or water is too thick and serve sprinkled with chopped mint and coriander.

Always give saffron a bash in a pestle and mortar, or crumble it between your fingers first. It is more expensive per gram than gold, so do leave it out if it's too pricey, but if you are going to commit, look out for Persian saffron – it may cost more, but it's the best quality.

SO MANY SOBA NOODLES

The two noodle dressings here go well with soba either hot or cold. They can also be used with spiralized sweet potatoes or other vegetables. The avocado sauce is a revelation.

COOK TIME: 5 MINS

250g **soba noodles**

1 teaspoon **rapeseed oil**

1. Cook the noodles in lots of boiling salted water for 5 minutes. Drain and toss in a little oil. See below for sauces to serve.

SESAME PEANUT SAUCE

PREP TIME: 10 MINS

4 tablespoons **toasted sesame seeds**

1 × 3cm piece of **ginger**, finely grated

2 cloves of **garlic**, crushed

4 **spring onions**, chopped

150g **smooth peanut butter**

3 tablespoons **tamari**

2 tablespoons **rice vinegar**

1 tablespoon **brown rice syrup**

2 teaspoons **chilli paste**

½ teaspoon **Sichuan peppercorns**, crushed

2 tablespoons **sesame oil**

150ml **water**

TO GARNISH

extra **toasted sesame seeds**

spring onions, chopped

1. Blend all the ingredients together until smooth.

2. Toss the cooked noodles with the sauce. The noodles can be eaten either hot or chilled, sprinkled with sesame seeds and spring onions.

AVOCADO SAUCE

PREP TIME: 10 MINS

2 **avocados**, chopped

juice of ½ **lemon**

1 clove of **garlic**, crushed

50ml **olive oil**, plus extra if needed

2 **red chillies**, chopped

2 tablespoons chopped **fresh parsley**

salt and **freshly ground black pepper**

1. Place the avocados in a blender with the lemon juice, garlic and olive oil.

2. Season well, adding a little water if needed so that the sauce has a coating consistency.

3. Toss the cooked noodles in the avocado sauce and sprinkle with the chopped chilli and parsley.

FRIDGE SOUP

This is a soup designed to use up all those salad bits and veg that generally end up being chucked out or don't look too special as they are particularly perishable.

PREP TIME: 10 MINS · COOK TIME: 25 MINS

2 tablespoons **olive oil**

1 **onion**, sliced

2 cloves of **garlic**, crushed

any herbs, such as **fresh basil**, **tarragon** or **chives**, chopped

¼ **cucumber**, sliced

4 **spring onions** or 1 **leek**, chopped

2 **potatoes**, peeled and thinly sliced

100g **mixed lettuce leaves** or 1 head of **lettuce**

800ml **vegetable stock**

chopped **fresh chives**

a pinch of **ground nutmeg**

salt and **freshly ground black pepper**

1. Heat the oil in a large pan and add the onion. Cook for 5 minutes, then add the garlic, herbs, cucumber, spring onions and sliced potatoes. Season well and cook for another 10 minutes, stirring to prevent the veg sticking.

2. Add the lettuce to the pan, ripping up any large leaves, and add the stock. Bring to the boil, then reduce the heat and simmer for 10 minutes, or until the potatoes are tender.

3. Blend the soup until smooth and check the seasoning, adding extra stock if the soup is too thick. For a very smooth result pass the soup through the finest setting of a food mill (mouli-legumes).

4. Serve with chopped chives and a little ground nutmeg.

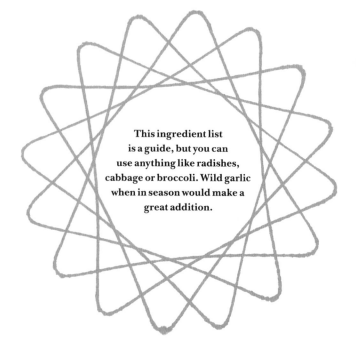

This ingredient list is a guide, but you can use anything like radishes, cabbage or broccoli. Wild garlic when in season would make a great addition.

EVERYDAY EASY

MUSHROOM BUN BURGERS

P
NF
SF

Who needs burger buns? One for the carnivores out there – the meaty consistency and taste of the field mushrooms is flipping fantastic. Do make sure you have plenty of kitchen roll on hand – these bad boys are so juicy that 'drippage' is unavoidable.

PREP TIME: 15 MINS · COOK TIME: 25 MINS

600g **veal mince** (or **pork**)

1 tablespoon chopped **fresh parsley**

1 tablespoon chopped **fresh chives**

zest of ½ **lemon**

1 clove of **garlic**, crushed

a dash of **chilli sauce**

2 **egg yolks**

8 **large field mushrooms**

2 tablespoons **olive oil**

1 **red onion**, sliced

4 **gherkins**, sliced

100g **baby salad leaves**

salt and **freshly ground black pepper**

1. Heat the oven to 160°C/325°F/gas mark 3.

2. Mix the mince with the herbs, lemon, garlic, chilli sauce and egg yolks. Season well and mix together. Shape into 4 patties and place in the refrigerator for a few hours.

3. Brush the field mushrooms with 1 tablespoon of oil and season. Bake in the oven for 15 minutes, until just tender.

4. Take the burgers out of the refrigerator 30 minutes before cooking. Heat a griddle pan and brush the burgers with oil. Grill for 4 minutes on each side. Leave to rest for a few minutes. Sandwich each burger between 2 mushrooms. Top with onion and gherkin slices. Serve with a green salad.

British rose veal comes from well-kept, grass-fed cows and is a more responsible way to enjoy veal meat.

TEA LEAF SALAD

Rather than the UK's traditional cuppa, this fermented tea leaf salad is a national favourite in Myanmar. Crunch, sweet, sour and savoury, it's a daily dish for the whole country, especially students – who use it as their version of Pro-Plus, because of its caffeine buzz. We're into it.

PREP TIME: 15 MINS · COOK TIME: 5 MINS · SOAK TIME: OVERNIGHT

3 tablespoons **split yellow peas**, soaked overnight

2 tablespoons **rice bran oil**

8 cloves of **garlic**, thinly sliced

3 tablespoons **fermented tea leaves**

1 tablespoons **dried shrimps**, chopped

1 **beefsteak tomato**, chopped

250g **cabbage**, very thinly sliced

2 tablespoons **roasted peanuts**

2 tablespoons **toasted sunflower seeds**

1 tablespoon **toasted sesame seeds**

1 tablespoon **lime juice**

1 **red chilli**, chopped

1 teaspoon **tamari**

TO SERVE

lime wedges (optional)

fresh coriander (optional)

1. Drain the split peas and fry in a tablespoon of the oil until lightly toasted. Remove from the pan and set aside. Heat the remaining oil in the pan, and fry the garlic slices until lightly browned.

2. Mix the split peas and garlic with the rest of the ingredients. Toss together and serve with lime wedges and coriander leaves, if liked.

SPROUTED BUCKWHEAT & SPROUT SALAD WITH SMOKED TROUT

Jane thought it would be funny to put something sprouted with sprouts. Sprouting the buckwheat does take a little love and attention, but is a great science experiment for the little ones.

PREP TIME: 10 MINS · SOAK TIME: 2 DAYS

100g **buckwheat**

juice of ½ **lemon**

3 tablespoons **olive oil**

2 teaspoons **maple syrup**

1 teaspoon **English mustard**

100g **Brussels sprouts**, shredded

50g **baby spinach leaves**

2 tablespoons chopped **fresh dill** (or **chives**)

2 tablespoons chopped **fresh mint**

400g **smoked trout** (or **cooked trout/salmon**)

handful of **wild garlic flowers**, to garnish (optional)

salt and **freshly ground black pepper**

1. Rinse the buckwheat well in lots of running cold water. Put into a bowl, cover with water and soak for about an hour. Drain, and spread the buckwheat in a fine sieve over a bowl. Cover with a clean damp cloth and leave at room temperature, rinsing the buckwheat twice a day with water until sprouts start to appear. Transfer to the refrigerator.

2. Whisk together the lemon juice, oil, maple syrup and mustard to make the dressing and season well.

3. In a large bowl, mix the buckwheat with the sprouts, spinach and herbs. Toss with the dressing. Pull apart the smoked trout into 2–3cm pieces and fold into the salad. Garnish with wild garlic flowers (if using) to serve.

4

SPEEDY SUPPERS

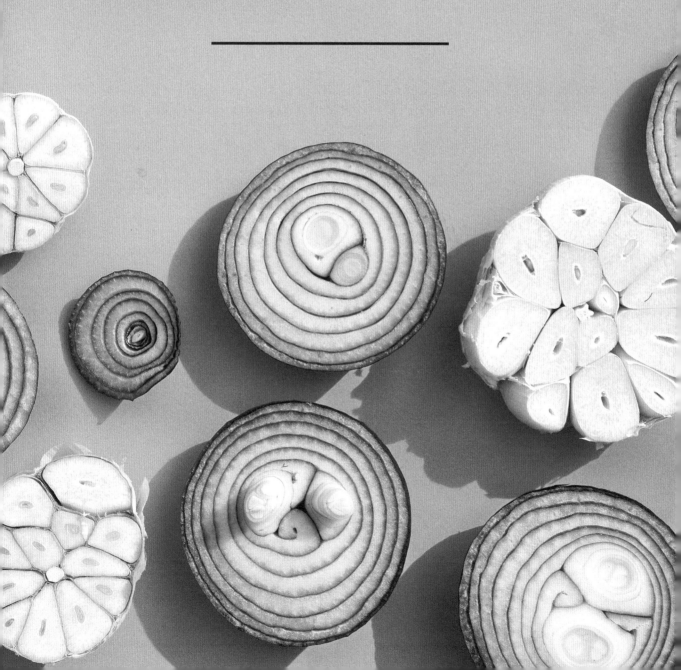

COCONUT WATER
FRIED CHICKEN

🍴 ④

This is a grown-up version of fried chicken.
The coconut water adds a delicacy to the dish that your guests will go nuts for.

PREP TIME: 30 MINS · COOK TIME: 15 MINS
MARINATING TIME: OVERNIGHT

400ml **coconut water**

1 clove of **garlic**, crushed

3 **shallots**, chopped

1 × 2cm cube of **ginger**, grated
   finely

2 **red chillies**, chopped

½ teaspoon **ground turmeric**

1 teaspoon **ground coriander**

1 teaspoon **salt**

8–10 **chicken thighs** (about 1.2kg)

rapeseed oil (or **vegetable oil**),
   for frying

75g **rice flour**

75g **cornflour**

sprigs of **fresh coriander**, to serve

½ a **lime**, to serve

1. Roughly blend the coconut water with the garlic, shallots, ginger, chillies and spices. Place the chicken in a shallow container and pour over the coconut spice mix. Massage it with your hands until it's well coated. Cover and leave to marinate overnight.

2. Place the chicken and its marinade in a large pan. Bring to the boil, then simmer over a low heat for about 20 minutes. Turn off the heat and allow the chicken to cool down in the marinade. At this point the chicken can sit in the refrigerator, still in the marinade, until needed.

3. Heat about 4–5cm of oil in a pan until it's about 180°C, or until a piece of bread dropped into the oil turns brown.

4. Mix together the 2 flours and tip on to a shallow tray or plate. Remove the chicken from the marinade and toss in the flour. Gently lower the chicken into the hot oil with a slotted spoon and fry for about 10–15 minutes over a medium heat, until golden brown. It is best to do 3 or 4 thighs at a time. Overcrowding the pan will only result in the temperature of the oil dropping, with the result that the chicken will stew in the oil. Remove from the oil with a slotted spoon and place on kitchen paper. Keep warm while you fry the rest of the chicken. Serve with coriander and a squeeze of lime.

Any leftover marinade makes a great base for a spicy chicken noodle soup.

LEON'S GFC
(Gluten-free Fried Chicken)

In the LEON development kitchen, we have spent a long time trying to perfect our gluten-free fried chicken. We think we've finally nailed it with this tempura-style batter, which doesn't compromise on crunch. The colder the fizzy water, the better. Batter than the dirty version.

PREP TIME: 10 MINS · COOK TIME: 10 MINS

6 **chicken thighs**, cut into small dice or strips

oil, for frying

FOR THE BATTER

60g **cornflour**

60g **gram flour** (or other **GF flour**)

1 **egg yolk**

180ml **sparkling water**

2 tablespoons **ground almonds**

1 tablespoon **mustard powder**

1 tablespoon **dried oregano**

1 tablespoon **chilli powder**

½ tablespoon **onion powder**

½ tablespoon **salt**

½ tablespoon **freshly ground black pepper**

mayonnaise and roughly chopped **tarragon**, to serve

1. Vigorously whisk the flours, egg yolk, sparkling water, ground almonds and mustard powder together, then stir in the spices and seasoning.

2. Coat the chicken in the batter and shallow-fry for 5 minutes, turning halfway, until golden and cooked through.

3. Place on kitchen paper to soak up excess oil, season to taste and serve with mayo (check that there's no added sugar) mixed with tarragon for dipping.

For a change, try adding the spices to oats or gluten-free cornflakes instead of making the batter.

(✓)
(P)
(NF)
(SF)

CHICKEN, LEMON & OLIVE TAGINE

This recipe, developed by Kay Plunkett-Hogge, has been our most popular seasonal stew on the LEON menu in years. It's summer in a stew.

PREP TIME: 15 MINS · MARINATING TIME: 1 HOUR · COOK TIME: 1 HOUR

500g **chicken thighs**, skinless and boneless, cut into 2cm cubes
¼ teaspoon **ground ginger**
½ teaspoon **freshly ground black pepper**
1 stick of **cinnamon**
a good pinch of **saffron**
2 teaspoons **ground cumin**
½ teaspoon **ground turmeric**
1 teaspoon **ras el hanout**
3 tablespoons **olive oil**
1 **onion**, peeled and chopped
3 cloves of **garlic**, crushed
200ml **chicken stock**
1 tablespoon **preserved lemon brine**
120g **pitted green olives**
1 **preserved lemon**, deseeded and chopped
4–6 tablespoons chopped **fresh parsley**, to serve
salt and **freshly ground black pepper**

1. Marinate the chicken with the dry spices and 1 tablespoon of olive oil for an hour.

2. Cook the onion and garlic in the remaining olive oil until just soft and turning golden.

3. Add the chicken and stir until combined. Add the stock and the preserved lemon brine, bring to the boil, then simmer, covered, for 35 minutes.

4. Now add the olives and preserved lemon, and taste for seasoning. Simmer for a further 5 minutes. Remove the chicken and olives and cook the sauce for a further 3–5 minutes to reduce. Shred the chicken cubes into strips.

5. Add the chicken and olives back into the sauce to very briefly bring everything together, then serve with a parsley garnish.

Add chickpeas to bulk out the chicken if you're on a budget. We like to serve this in our restaurants on a bed of brown rice with a wedge of fresh lemon.

TURKEY SAN CHOY BAU

These little Chinese lettuce parcels are such an easy one-pot supper. We've used turkey here because it's lean, but swap it for chicken, pork or tofu if you prefer.

PREP TIME: 15 MINS · COOK TIME: 10 MINS

1 tablespoon **rice bran oil**

1 clove of **garlic**, crushed

1 × 2cm piece of **ginger**, finely grated

300g **turkey breast**, chopped

100g **shiitake mushrooms**, chopped

4 **water chestnuts**, cut into thin needles

2 teaspoons **Sichuan peppercorns**, crushed

2 tablespoons **tamari**, plus extra to serve

6 **spring onions**, chopped

50g **rice noodles** (optional)

oil, for deep-frying (optional)

salt and **freshly ground black pepper**

TO SERVE

3 **Little Gem** or 1 **iceberg lettuce**

½ **cucumber**, deseeded and thinly sliced

sugar-free chilli sauce (optional)

a handful of **beansprouts**

1. Heat the oil in a wok or frying pan. Add the garlic, ginger and turkey and stir-fry for 3 minutes. Add the mushrooms, water chestnuts, peppercorns and tamari. Cook for another 2–3 minutes, then season and add half the spring onions. Set aside.

2. If using the noodles, heat the oil to 180°C and fry them until crisp. Drain on kitchen paper.

3. Break up the noodles and mix with the turkey mushroom mix and the rest of the spring onions. Transfer to a serving dish.

4. Serve with the lettuce leaves, cucumber, tamari, beansprouts and chilli sauce, if using. This is a fun one for little hands to make their own parcels.

SALT-N-PEPA SQUID

Push it, push it real good.

PREP TIME: 15 MINS · COOK TIME: 15 MINS

cornflour, to coat

rapeseed oil, for deep-frying

200g **French beans** and **runner beans**, trimmed

200g **squid pieces** and tentacles, cleaned

1 tablespoon **rapeseed oil**

4 cloves of **garlic**, thinly sliced

2 **red chillies**, sliced

4 **spring onions**, sliced

salt and **freshly ground black pepper**

FOR THE BATTER

2 tablespoons **potato starch**

2 tablespoons **tapioca flour**

2 tablespoons **arrowroot**

1 teaspoon **Sichuan peppercorns**, ground

a large pinch of **salt**

about 100ml **soda water**

a pinch of **bicarbonate of soda**

1. Sieve together the potato starch, tapioca and arrowroot. Stir in the salt and pepper. Pour in soda water, whisking until you have a thin batter, then add a large pinch of bicarbonate of soda.

2. Pour a few tablespoons of cornflour on to a plate and season.

3. Heat the oil for deep-frying to about 180°C. You will need to deep-fry the beans and squid in batches – first toss them in the cornflour, then quickly dredge in the batter and fry for a few minutes until crisp.

4. While the beans and squid are frying, heat the tablespoon of flaxseed oil in a non-stick frying pan and cook the garlic and chillies for a few minutes, until the garlic is golden brown. Add the spring onions at the last minute and toss together. Drain on kitchen paper.

5. When all the beans and squid are cooked, serve on a dish sprinkled with the garlic, chillies and spring onions.

Use flaxseed oil instead of rapeseed oil if you want to make this paleo.

RUNNER BEAN PASTA

4

In Puglia, Jane went to a farmhouse near Ostuni called Il Frantoio. The food there is all very vegetable based and they serve a dish using 'fagiolini di mezzometro' or 'half metre beans', where the beans are dressed with a tomato sauce and look very much like a thick pasta. No need to do a runner and escape to Puglia, we've brought the recipe to you.

PREP TIME: 10 MINS · COOK TIME: 2–3 MINS

500g **runner beans**, trimmed and cut into thin long strips

1. Trim the beans and slice into long thin strips – a bean slicer will do this for you (or recruit a bean slicer AKA partner, to help).

2. Cook in lots of boiling salted water for 2 minutes. Drain and toss with one of the following sauces to serve.

VONGOLE

PREP TIME: 10 MINS · COOK TIME: 10 MINS

1kg **clams**
100ml **white wine**
3 cloves of **garlic**, 1 crushed and 2 chopped
2 tablespoons **olive oil**
2 **red chillies**, chopped
2 tablespoons chopped **fresh parsley**
extra virgin olive oil

1. Heat a large pan until very hot. Add the clams along with the wine and crushed garlic. Shake the pan, cover and leave to cook for 2–3 minutes, or until the clams have started to open. Drain the clams in a colander over a bowl to collect the cooking liquor.

2. Heat the olive oil in a large pan and add the chopped garlic and chillies. Cook for a minute, then add the clam cooking liquor. Cook over a high heat until it has reduced enough to coat the back of your wooden spoon.

3. Add the cooked runner beans to the pan along with the cooked clams. Toss together with the chopped parsley and serve drizzled with extra virgin olive oil.

SALT COD, TOMATO & PARSLEY

PREP TIME: 10 MINS · COOK TIME: 5 MINS

2 tablespoons **olive oil**
1 **clove** of garlic, crushed
1 **red chilli**, finely chopped
4 **anchovy fillets**
15 **cherry tomatoes**, quartered
2 tablespoons chopped **fresh parsley**
200g **cooked salt cod**, flaked
a drizzle of **extra virgin olive oil**
salt and **freshly ground black pepper**

1. Heat the olive oil in a large pan. Add the garlic and chilli and cook over a medium heat for a minute (careful not to colour the garlic). Take off the heat and add the anchovies, beating vigorously until they 'melt' into the oil.

2. Drain the cooked runner beans and add to the anchovy and chilli oil, tossing until the beans are well coated.

3. Fold in the tomatoes, parsley and salt cod and season well. Serve drizzled with extra virgin olive oil.

CARBONARA

If you're making the Carbonara sauce, just use the prepped beans raw as they will cook in the sauce.

PREP TIME: 10 MINS · COOK TIME: 15 MINS

2 tablespoons **olive oil**

4 cloves of **garlic**

200g **pancetta lardons** (or **sliced pancetta**)

2 **eggs**

1 **egg yolk**

1 tablespoon chopped **fresh parsley**

1 tablespoon chopped **fresh chives**

salt and **freshly ground black pepper**

1. Heat the oil in a frying pan and gently cook the garlic for 3 minutes over a medium heat until the garlic starts to turn brown. Remove from the pan and tip in the pancetta. Cook for about 5 minutes, until the pancetta is golden.

2. Whisk the eggs and yolk together.

3. Bring a large pan of well-salted water to the boil. Drop in your (raw) runner beans and cook for about 3 minutes, or until the beans are tender. Drain and reserve a couple of tablespoons of cooking water.

4. Add a tablespoon of the cooking water to the eggs and whisk together. Return the runners to the pan while still hot. Tip in the pancetta, with the fat too. Stir well and add the egg mix. Make sure the pan is off the heat (you don't want scrambled eggs) and fold through until all the bean strips are coated. Season well with black pepper and serve topped with the herbs.

If the sauce seems too dry, add some extra cooking water until it is the desired consistency.

MUSSEL & SMOKED SALMON

PREP TIME: 10 MINS
COOK TIME: 15 MINS

500g **mussels**, cleaned
2 cloves of **garlic**, crushed
100ml **white wine**
1 tablespoon **olive oil**
1 tablespoon chopped **fresh rosemary**
1 **red pepper**, finely diced
100g **smoked salmon**, chopped

1. Heat a pan until very hot. Tip in the mussels with the garlic and white wine, give the pan a shake, and cover. Cook for 2–3 minutes, or until the mussels have just opened. Pour the mussels into a colander over a bowl, to collect the cooking liquor.

2. Heat the oil in a pan and cook the rosemary with the red pepper for about 5 minutes. Add the mussel liquor and reduce by half.

3. While the sauce is reducing, pick the mussels from the shells. Add the mussels with the chopped smoked salmon to the reduced sauce and toss with the cooked runner beans.

AUBERGINE, TOMATO, OLIVE & BASIL

PREP TIME: 10 MINS
COOK TIME: 50 MINS

2 **aubergines**
3 tablespoons **olive oil**
5 cloves of **garlic**, finely sliced
a pinch of **chilli flakes**
1 × 440g tin of **chopped tomatoes**
2 teaspoons **balsamic vinegar**
1 tablespoon **black olives**, chopped
1 tablespoon **capers**
2 tablespoons shredded **fresh basil**
a drizzle of **extra virgin olive oil**
salt and **freshly ground black pepper**

1. Chop the aubergine into 1–2cm chunks. Heat the olive oil in a large pan and brown the aubergine in batches, cooking each batch for about 5 minutes. Don't cook them all at once, or they won't brown.

2. Remove from the pan with a slotted spoon and drain on kitchen paper.

3. Add the garlic and chilli flakes to the pan. Cook for a minute, then add the tinned tomatoes. Simmer the sauce for about 20–30 minutes, or until it has reduced. Add the vinegar and return the browned aubergines to the pan. Cook for another 10 minutes over a low heat.

4. Add the olives, capers and basil. Check the seasoning and toss with the cooked beans. Drizzle with good extra virgin olive oil to serve.

BLACK & WHITE SQUID

This visually stunning stir-fry is tender, while retaining lots of satisfying crunch. The trick with squid is to cook it very, very quickly – this isn't a dish to turn your back on.

PREP TIME: 30 MINS · COOK TIME: 7 MINS

600g **squid**, cleaned

1 head of **fennel**

1 **red onion**, thinly sliced

2 **courgettes**

1 **red pepper**

100g **runner beans**

2 tablespoons **olive oil**

1 packet of **squid ink**

2 **red chillies**, finely chopped

2 tablespoons chopped **fresh flat-leaf parsley**

1 clove of **garlic**, crushed

3 tablespoons **extra virgin olive oil**

salt and **freshly ground black pepper**

1. Slice the squid bodies into long thin strips. Cut the tentacles into similar-size pieces. Set aside.

2. Slice all the vegetables into long thin strips of similar size. Heat a tablespoon of olive oil in a large frying pan or wok until very hot. Tip in the veg and fry quickly for a few minutes, until just cooked. Season well and tip on to a serving platter.

3. Heat the remaining oil in the pan until very hot. Tip in half the squid and cook for about 30 seconds, stirring well. Season and remove from the pan with a slotted spoon to another dish. While the pan is still hot, add the other half of the squid and fry quickly for a few seconds, then add the squid ink. Cook for about 20 seconds, so the squid is coated and hot.

4. Spoon the black squid on top of the vegetables and the white squid on top of that.

5. Mix the chillies, parsley and garlic with the extra virgin olive oil and drizzle over the squid to serve.

BRAZILIAN BLACK BEAN STEW

Our version of the traditional Brazilian feijoada. It tastes decadent while being remarkably good for you. It's so hearty and filling that when Adam, John's best friend and our property director at LEON, first tried this new vegan dish, he said, 'I love that new meaty one.'

PREP TIME: 15 MINS · COOK TIME: 40 MINS

1 large **onion**, roughly chopped

2 tablespoons **rapeseed oil**

1 **carrot**, chopped into rounds

1 stick of **celery**, chopped

½ **leek**, chopped

1 **bay leaf**

1 teaspoon **tomato purée**

1 teaspoon **sweet paprika**

½ teaspoon **smoked paprika**

1 teaspoon **chipotle sauce**

1 teaspoon **dried oregano**

350g **black beans**, cooked

300ml **vegetable stock**

1 clove of **garlic**, crushed

1 tablespoon **tamari**

1 teaspoon **red wine vinegar**

salt and **freshly ground black pepper**

1 tablespoon chopped **fresh coriander**, to garnish

1. In a large pan, cook the onion in the oil for 5 minutes over a medium heat. Add the carrot, celery, leek and bay leaf. Stir well and cook gently for about 20 minutes, without browning the vegetables.

2. Add the tomato purée, spices and herbs and cook for another 5 minutes, stirring well to combine.

3. Add the beans, stock, garlic, tamari and vinegar. Turn up the heat and cook until the sauce has thickened to coat the beans and vegetables. Season well to and serve sprinkled with coriander.

We serve our stew with brown rice and a little fresh coriander sprinkled on top.

FISH FINGERS WITH
A SESAME COCONUT CRUST

Consider these fancy fish fingers. Any firm white fish works well, like gurnard, bream or bass.
Another one bites the crust.

PREP TIME: 10 MINS · COOK TIME: 10 MINS

4 × 150g **firm white fish fillets**,
   skinned

2 teaspoons **wasabi paste**

3 tablespoon **rice bran oil**

wilted spinach or **rainbow chard**,
   to serve

a squeeze of **lime juice**, to serve

salt and **cayenne pepper**

FOR THE PASTE

1 teaspoon **palm sugar**

1 **egg**, beaten

1 tablespoon **tamari**

3 tablespoons **sesame seeds**

2 tablespoons **desiccated coconut**

2 tablespoons chopped **fresh
   coriander**

1 clove of **garlic**, crushed

1. Heat the oven to 150°C/300°F/gas mark 2.

2. Mix the paste ingredients together in a bowl and put to one side.

3. Season the fish well and leave for 15 minutes. Dry with kitchen paper and spread a little wasabi on one side of each fillet. Press the paste on to each fillet, on top of the wasabi.

4. Heat the oil in an ovenproof frying pan. Gently fry the fish fillets, paste side down, for 3 minutes, or until the crust is browned. Carefully flip them over and transfer the pan to the oven. Cook for about 5 minutes. The cooking time may vary depending on the thickness and type of fish used.

5. Serve with wilted spinach or rainbow chard and a squeeze of lime.

This can be served
with braised kale or
lentils. If you're not a fan
of fish, the crust works
just as well
on chicken.

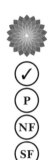

LAMB & ROASTED SUMMER VEGETABLES

Jane ate this very simple dish at Trattoria La Madia in Lombardy. A friend of hers, Christine Smallwood, was there to interview the chef for her book about the region. Jane was there to crash a bunch of photoshoots while on a camping trip. Roasting vegetables is not just for winter roots – any vegetables can be used, just add the veg that take less time to cook 5 minutes before serving.

PREP TIME: 20 MINS · COOK TIME: 40 MINS

500g **mixed vegetables** (to include **cauliflower, romanesco, radishes, fennel, courgettes, turnips, baby carrots, beans, peas** and **cabbage**)

3 tablespoons **olive oil**

2 cloves of **garlic**, crushed

3 tablespoons chopped **fresh herbs** (**chives, tarragon** and **chervil**)

300g **lamb loin** or **lamb leg steaks**, trimmed

salt and **freshly ground black pepper**

1. Heat the oven to 180°C/350°F/gas mark 4.

2. Cut the cauliflower and romanesco into small florets, halve the radishes, slice the fennel, and chop the courgettes and turnips. Toss in 2 tablespoons of the olive oil with the garlic and herbs. Place on a baking tray and put into the oven. Roast for about 25 minutes, giving them a stir after 15 minutes.

3. Meanwhile, cut the rest of the vegetables into small pieces except the peas and cabbage. Add them all to the tray and cook for another 5 minutes.

4. While the veg are cooking, season the lamb loins and pan-fry in a tablespoon of olive oil for about 6 minutes, turning frequently until slightly firm to touch. Allow to rest for at least 5 minutes.

5. Slice the lamb thinly and fold into the vegetables before serving.

SOLE & GRAPE SALAD

A salad so light and fresh it gives you grape expectations for a British summer.

PREP TIME: 15 MINS · COOK TIME: 5 MINS

300g **megrim sole fillets**, skinned

1 teaspoon **cayenne pepper**

100g **grapes** (peeled if you have the time)

2 **shallots**, sliced

leaves from a small bunch of **fresh tarragon**

10 **radishes**, quartered

¼ **cucumber**, peeled, deseeded and cut into thin slices

70g **lamb's lettuce** or **pea shoots**

FOR THE DRESSING

50g **white grapes**

2 tablespoons **moscatel vinegar**

4 tablespoons **grapeseed oil**

salt and **freshly ground black pepper**

1. Trim the fish fillets. Place on a plate and sprinkle with about ½ teaspoon of salt. Cover and place in the refrigerator.

2. Cut the grapes in half and mix with the shallots, tarragon, radishes and cucumber.

3. Make the dressing by blending all the ingredients together, then passing through a sieve. Season well.

4. Take the fish out of the refrigerator and dry with kitchen paper. Place on a clean plate and sprinkle with cayenne. Put the plate in a steamer and steam for about 5 minutes, or until the fish is just firm.

5. Arrange the grapes, shallots, cucumber, radishes and herbs on a plate with the lamb's lettuce. Top with the sole fillets and drizzle with the dressing to serve.

To peel your grapes easily, cover them with boiling water and leave for a few minutes, then drain and peel.

JERK PORK

Don't be a jerk, make a jerk. Serve it in a corn tortilla or flat bread (pages 248 and 250).

PREP TIME: 15 MINS · MARINATING TIME: OVERNIGHT · COOK TIME: 10 MINS

1.2kg **pork fillet**

corn tortillas, (see page 248), to serve

FOR THE MARINADE

6 **red chillies**, finely chopped

3 cloves of **garlic**, crushed

1 bunch of **spring onions**, chopped

1 × 3cm piece of **ginger**, finely grated

2 tablespoons **sambal oelek** – or make your own (see hoppers toppers, page 40)

50ml **rice bran oil**

2 tablespoons **rice vinegar**

1 teaspoon **ground allspice**

50ml **tamari**

salt and **freshly ground black pepper**

FOR THE PINEAPPLE SALSA

½ **pineapple**, peeled and cut into small dice

1 **red chilli**, deseeded and finely chopped

1 tablespoon **coriander**, chopped

juice from 1 **lime**

salt and **freshly ground black pepper**

1. Trim the pork fillet, removing any sinew, and slice across the fillet, on the diagonal, into pieces 1–2cm thick.

2. Put all the marinade ingredients into a food processor and blend until smooth. Place in a container with the meat and rub the marinade into the pork. If you can, leave overnight in the refrigerator.

3. Mix all the ingredients for the pineapple salsa together, season, and set aside.

4. Heat a heavy-based griddle pan (or a barbecue) until very hot. Grill the pork fillet pieces for 2 minutes on each side, until almost firm to touch. The pork can be served slightly pink. This can be done in batches, with the cooked pork held in a warm dish until ready to serve.

5. Any remaining marinade can be simmered with a little water for 10 minutes and poured over the pork. Serve in a corn tortilla with the pineapple salsa.

This would also work with stuffed sweet potatoes (see page 100) and a green salad. The marinade also goes well with beef or chicken.

LEON LAMB KOFTE

Kofte load of these. Another staple on the LEON menu, we use them either in a wrap (a prima doner), on a superfood salad base, or with chilli sauce on brown rice as meatballs. It's totally up to you. The word kofte means 'to beat', so let it all out when you mix – it should be really bashed around and tenderized.

PREP TIME: 15 MINS · COOK TIME: 10 MINS

500g **lamb mince**

large handfuls of chopped **fresh oregano** and **thyme**

½ teaspoon each of **ground cumin**, **coriander**, **cloves** and **cardamom**

1 teaspoon **yellow mustard seeds**

1 teaspoon **red chilli flakes**

3 cloves of **garlic**, crushed

salt and **freshly ground black pepper**

1 tablespoon **olive oil**

1. Heat the oven to 200°C/400°F/gas mark 6.

2. Mix all the ingredients except for the oil together. Bash it all together with your hands to combine thoroughly. Roll into egg-size balls.

3. Heat the oil in a frying pan, add the kofte to brown them and get the outside caramelized. After 4–5 minutes, transfer them to a thick-bottomed baking tray for 7–10 minutes, until cooked through. Drain on kitchen paper before serving.

Serve with some salad leaves, semi-dried and baby plum tomatoes, good-quality hummus, sauerkraut, pomegranate seeds and chilli sauce.

ROAST CHICKEN WITH JERUSALEM ARTICHOKES & COPPA DI PARMA

An impressive one-pot roast. Knobbly, nutty Jerusalem artichokes have nothing to do with Jerusalem, or with artichokes. They're in season from November to March – make the most of it. They are brilliant.

PREP TIME: 15 MINS · COOK TIME: 40 MINS

600g **Jerusalem artichokes**, peeled

4 **leeks**, sliced

20 **fresh sage leaves**, shredded

100g **coppa di Parma slices**

500ml **strong chicken stock**

1 clove of **garlic**, crushed

6–8 **chicken thighs**, skin on and bone in

salt and **freshly ground black pepper**

1. Heat the oven to 180°C/350°F/gas mark 4.

2. Slice the artichokes into rounds about 1cm thick. Layer in the bottom of an ovenproof dish with the leeks, sage and coppa di Parma, seasoning each layer.

3. Mix the stock with the garlic and pour over the artichokes and leeks.

4. Place a wire rack (from a grill pan) over the ovenproof dish. Season the chicken pieces and place on the rack, skin side up, so that any juices drip on to the vegetables below.

5. Place in the oven and roast for about 40 minutes, or until the chicken is cooked through and the artichokes are tender. Leave to cool slightly before serving.

ASIAN FISH BROTH

This broth will banish any colds or flus that may be brewing in your home. Use the spice paste with chicken for a chicken broth, too.

PREP TIME: 15 MINS · COOK TIME: 15 MINS

300ml **coconut water**

400ml **fish stock**

2 stalks of **lemongrass**, chopped

2 **shallots**, sliced

400g **firm white fish fillets**, skin removed

200g **beansprouts**

100g **sugar snaps**, sliced

juice of 2 **limes**

1 **red chilli**, sliced

leaves from a small bunch of **Thai basil**

salt and **freshly ground black pepper**

FOR THE PASTE

1 × 2cm piece of **ginger**, grated

2 cloves of **garlic**, crushed

2 **red chillies**, finely chopped

1 teaspoon **ground turmeric**

2 tablespoons chopped **fresh coriander stalks**

1 bunch of **spring onions**, chopped

25g **creamed coconut**, grated

½ teaspoon **salt**

1. Blend together the paste ingredients in a food processor until smooth.

2. Heat the coconut water with the fish stock, lemongrass and shallots. Whisk in the paste and simmer for about 10 minutes.

3. Add the fish to the broth and cook over a low heat for about 5 minutes, until the fish is just cooked. The cooking time will be dependent on the thickness of the fillets.

4. Place the beansprouts and sugar snaps in a large serving bowl. Add lime juice to the broth to taste, and check the seasoning. Ladle the soup over the beansprouts. Sprinkle with the chilli and basil leaves to serve.

You can buy Thai basil frozen from Asian supermarkets. If you can't find it, don't worry, sprinkle with coriander leaves (just not regular basil, it doesn't make a good swap).

DEVILLED CALVES' LIVER WITH KALE & PANCETTA

Liver and bacon are a heavenly devilled pair.
We could make more jokes, but you'd think they were offal.

PREP TIME: 20 MINS · COOK TIME: 45 MINS

4 tablespoons **olive oil**

4 **red onions**, sliced

200g **kale**

100g **pancetta lardons**

1 clove of **garlic**, crushed

1 × 400g tin of **borlotti beans**,
  drained and rinsed

400g **calves' liver** slices, trimmed

1 tablespoon **balsamic vinegar**

2 tablespoons chopped **fresh
  chives**

salt and **freshly ground black
  pepper**

FOR THE DEVILLED SAUCE

1 **shallot**

1 tablespoon **olive oil**

1 clove of **garlic**, crushed

50ml **white wine**

100ml **chicken stock**

2 teaspoons **English mustard**

2 teaspoons **Dijon mustard**

2 teaspoons **tomato purée**

a dash of **gluten-free
  Worcestershire sauce**

a dash of **Tabasco**

1 teaspoon **maple syrup**

1. Heat 2 tablespoons of oil in a large pan. Add the sliced onions and cook over a low heat for at least 30 minutes. The longer you can cook them for, the sweeter they will be. Season well.

2. While the onions are cooking, make the devilled sauce. Cook the shallot in the olive oil for 5 minutes. Add the garlic and wine, turn up the heat and reduce to a syrup. Add the stock with the rest of the ingredients, whisk together and simmer for 5 minutes.

3. Remove the central rib from the kale and discard. Blanch the leaves in plenty of boiling salted water for 2 minutes. Drain, refresh in cold water and squeeze out any excess liquid. Roughly chop the kale.

4. Heat 1 tablespoon of oil in a pan and cook the pancetta lardons until lightly browned. Add the garlic, cook for a minute, then stir in the kale. Braise for a few minutes, then stir in the borlotti beans. Cook for a few minutes to heat through and season well.

5. Heat the last tablespoon of oil in a large non-stick pan and cook the calves' liver for a minute on either side. The liver should be slightly pink in the middle. The cooking time will depend on the thickness of the slices. Add a splash of balsamic vinegar and season. Remove the liver from the pan and add the devilled sauce to heat through.

6. To serve, spoon the kale and beans on to plates with the liver. Top with the onions and devilled sauce, and sprinkle with chopped chives to serve.

CELERIAC PASTA

4

Celeriac can be cut into tagliatelle-like pasta strips, or you can try spiralizing it (but it's quite a workout!) – the best thing to do is use a mandolin to cut it into large rounds, then to slice with a knife. We cannot emphasize enough how brilliant a replacement for pasta this is. It doesn't taste remotely like celeriac once cooked and coated in these sauces. Serve it to a gluten-eater and they'd be none-the-wiser. Promise.

PREP TIME: 10 MINS · COOK TIME: 3 MINS

1 large **celeriac**, peeled

1 tablespoon **olive oil**

salt and **freshly ground black pepper**

1. Cut the celeriac into very thin slices, using a mandolin if you have one. Cut each slice into strips about 1–2cm wide, or into rough triangles.

2. Cook in a large pan of boiling water for 3 minutes, then drain well and toss with the olive oil. Season very well.

3. Toss with one of the following pasta sauces to serve.

1. CAPER, HERB & EGG DRESSING

PREP TIME: 15 MINS

2 tablespoons **salted capers**, soaked in **cold water**

2 tablespoons **gherkins**, chopped

2 tablespoons **fresh tarragon**, chopped

2 tablespoons **fresh chives**, chopped

2 **shallots**, finely chopped

2 tablespoons **fresh parsley**, chopped

1 tablespoon **Dijon mustard**

1 tablespoon **grain mustard**

2 **egg yolks**

salt and **freshly ground black pepper**

1. Drain the capers and roughly chop. Mix with the rest of the ingredients. Season well.

2. When the celeriac is drained but while it's still hot, toss with the dressing off the heat.

2. SAUSAGE & TOMATO SAUCE

PREP TIME: 10 MINS · COOK TIME: 50 MINS

1 tablespoon **olive oil**

400g good-quality **gluten-free pork sausages**

2 teaspoons **ground fennel seeds**

a good pinch of **dried chilli flakes**

leaves from 1 sprig of **fresh rosemary**, chopped

5 cloves of **garlic**, finely sliced

600g tinned **chopped tomatoes**

salt and **freshly ground black pepper**

1. Heat the oil in a large shallow pan. Remove the sausage skins and crumble the meat into the pan. Brown for a few minutes, then push to one side. Add the fennel, chilli flakes, rosemary and garlic. Stir and cook for a minute, then tip in the tomatoes and stir everything together.

2. Bring to a simmer and cook over a low heat for about 45 minutes. Season well and toss with the celeriac.

3. LAMB & PEA SAUCE

PREP TIME: 10 MINS · COOK TIME: 1 HOUR 30 MINS

250g **lamb shoulder**, cut into 1cm
  cubes
1 tablespoon **olive oil**
1 **onion**, finely chopped
2 cloves of **garlic**, crushed
250ml **chicken** or **lamb stock**
1 tablespoon **red wine vinegar**
150g **peas**
a bunch of **fresh parsley**,
  shredded
salt and **freshly ground black
  pepper**

1. Fry the lamb in the oil until lightly browned. Add the onion and cook over a gentle heat for about 20 minutes. If the lamb is very fatty, pour away the excess fat.

2. Add the garlic and cook for a minute, then pour in the stock and vinegar. Season well, cover, and cook for about an hour, or until the lamb is tender.

3. Uncover the pan and reduce the sauce until thick. Add the peas and cook for a minute. Stir in the parsley and season.

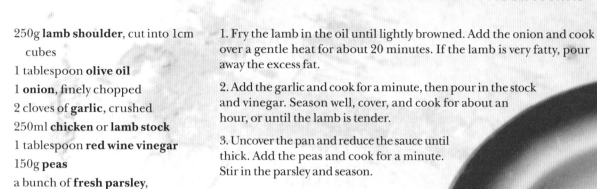

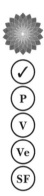

SWEET POTATO & OKRA STEW

A twist on the traditional West African groundnut stew. We use peanut butter, and it's magnificent. If okra isn't usually a staple vegetable in your house, buy a bunch of it and freeze it. It holds its shape well, and won't disintegrate.

PREP TIME: 15 MINS · COOK TIME: 35 MINS

1 tablespoon **coconut oil**

2 **onions**, finely chopped

2 cloves of **garlic**, crushed

1 × 2cm piece of **ginger**, grated

1 **red chilli**, chopped

2 **sweet potatoes**, peeled and cut into 1–2cm chunks

15 **okra**, sliced

1 teaspoon **ground cumin**

½ teaspoon **ground turmeric**

½ teaspoon **ground cinnamon**

1 teaspoon **smoked paprika**

3 large **tomatoes**, skinned and diced

350ml **vegetable stock**

100g **chard**, **kale** or **spring greens**, shredded

3 tablespoons **smooth peanut butter**

2 tablespoons crushed **unsalted peanuts**

2 tablespoons chopped **fresh coriander**

salt and **freshly ground black pepper**

1. Heat the oil in a large pan, add the onions and cook for 10 minutes. Stir in the garlic, ginger, chilli, sweet potatoes and sliced okra. Stir well and cook for 2 minutes, sprinkling the veg with the spices.

2. Add the diced tomatoes and season well. Pour in the stock and bring up to a simmer. Cook over a low heat for about 15 minutes, or until the sweet potato is tender.

3. Add the greens and cover the pan. Simmer for 2 minutes, or until the greens are tender. Stir in the peanut butter. Add a little extra stock if it seems too thick. Cook for another 5 minutes, then check the seasoning.

4. Serve sprinkled with crushed peanuts and chopped coriander.

This would be a good accompaniment to our Ehtiopian flat bread (see page 250).

PIZZA

Jo, who designed this book, is obsessed with pizza. She's got a pizza phone case and pizza socks. She's now obsessed with this. We made half into pissaladière and topped half with tomato sauce, griddled courgettes and chilli for a bit of variety. The paleo cauliflower base will steal a pizza your heart.

PREP TIME: 10 MINS · COOK TIME: 25 MINS

1 small **cauliflower**

1 tablespoon **olive oil**

100g **almond flour** (or **ground almonds**)

2 **eggs**

1 teaspoon **nutritional yeast** (or similar, optional)

salt and **freshly ground black pepper**

1. Heat the oven to 200°C/400°F/gas mark 6.

2. To make the base, remove the florets from the cauliflower and blitz in a food processor until they resemble couscous. Heat the oil in a large shallow pan and fry the cauliflower for about 5 minutes, stirring well.

3. Allow the cauliflower to cool, then place in a food processor with the other ingredients and season well. Blitz to combine, then turn out on to a baking tray lined with baking parchment. With a spatula or your fingers, spread the mix out to make a circle (about 30cm wide) or a rectangle – try to make it about 0.5cm deep.

4. Bake in the oven for about 20 minutes, or until it starts to turn golden brown. Remove from the oven and set to one side while you make the topping.

PISSALADIÈRE

PREP TIME: 10 MINS · COOK TIME: 55 MINS

3 tablespoons **olive oil**

3 **onions**, thinly sliced

3 **red onions**, thinly sliced

a sprig of **fresh thyme**

1 **bay leaf**

1 clove of **garlic**, crushed

10 **anchovy fillets** in oil

8 **baby plum tomatoes**, sliced

15 **black olives**, stoned

salt

1. Heat the oil in a large shallow pan. Add all the onions, sprinkle with a little salt, add the thyme and bay leaf, and cook gently over a low heat for about 40 minutes without browning.

2. Add the garlic and 3 of the anchovies and cook for a few minutes, or until the anchovies have melted into the onions.

3. Spread the onions over the pizza base and arrange the remaining anchovies, sliced tomatoes and black olives on top.

4. Put the pissaladière back into the oven for 10 minutes to finish cooking.

OTHER SERVING IDEAS

tomato sauce (see page 88) with grilled **aubergines**, **olives** and **oregano**

slow-cooked **leeks**, **prosciutto** and **sage**

courgettes, **peppers**, **mint** and **capers**

SPRING CHICKEN

This chicken with spring vegetables, dumplings and tarragon gremolata is not no spring chicken.

PREP TIME: 15 MINS · COOK TIME: 30 MINS

4 **chicken breasts**

1 tablespoon **olive oil**

500ml **chicken stock**

8 small **carrots**, peeled

8 **baby turnips**, peeled

8 **baby leeks** or **spring onions**, trimmed

100g **broad beans**

100g **asparagus**, cut into 2cm pieces

100g **peas**

salt and **freshly ground black pepper**

FOR THE DUMPLINGS

3 tablespoons **arrowroot**

75g toasted **ground almonds**

a pinch of **bicarbonate of soda**

½ teaspoon **salt**

about 80ml **chicken stock**, plus extra for poaching

FOR THE GREMOLATA

1 tablespoon chopped **fresh parsley**

1 tablespoon chopped **fresh tarragon**

very fine zest of 2 **lemons**

2 cloves of **garlic**, very finely chopped

1. Season the chicken breasts with salt and pepper. Heat the oil in a large pan and put the chicken in skin side down. Cook for a few minutes, or until the skin is lightly browned. Turn over and seal the other side for 2 minutes.

2. Pour in the stock and bring up to a simmer. Add the carrots and turnips and cook gently for 5 minutes with the chicken. Add the rest of the vegetables and cook for 5 minutes. Turn off the heat and allow to rest. Check the chicken is firm to touch and cooked through.

3. Mix together the arrowroot, almonds, bicarbonate of soda and salt in a bowl. Slowly add the stock until you have a wet but manageable dough (it will be on the wet side of manageable). Let the mixture stand for 15 minutes to thicken. Roll into small balls about 2cm in diameter if you can, but you may find it easier to use two spoons to make quenelles (think of a fancy ice cream scoop).

4. Heat the extra chicken stock in a small pan to the depth of 2cm. When it's simmering, add the dumplings and poach for 10 minutes over a low heat. Add to the chicken.

5. Mix together the parsley, tarragon, lemon zest and garlic. Sprinkle over the chicken and vegetables just before serving.

You could easily make this an autumn chicken with seasonal veg.

FEIJOADA SOUP

Feijoada is a Brazilian stew made with different cuts of pork: smoked, fatty and extremities. You can use a pressure cooker to speed up the cooking of the meat. Pre-cooking a smoked ham hock results in really good stock that you can use in the soup.

PREP TIME: 20 MINS · COOK TIME: 1 HOUR 20 MINS

1 tablespoon **olive oil**

75g **pancetta lardons**

200g **cooking chorizo**, cut into chunks

300g **pork shoulder**, cut into 2cm dice

300g **pork ribs**

1 **red chilli**, chopped

3 **onions**, chopped

1 **red pepper**, chopped

4 cloves of **garlic**, crushed

2 **bay leaves**

a pinch of **dried thyme**

2 teaspoons **smoked paprika**

2 strips of **orange zest**

1 litre **chicken or ham stock**, plus extra for thinning

1 × 400g tin of **black beans**

150g **edamame beans**

100g flaked **ham hock** (optional)

100g **kale**

2 teaspoons **red wine vinegar**

salt and **freshly ground black pepper**

FOR THE FAROFA

50ml **olive oil**

1 **onion**, finely chopped

200g **cassava flour**

a pinch of **salt**

1. Heat the oil in a large pan and add the lardons and chorizo. Cook over a medium heat for 5 minutes, until lightly browned. Remove with a slotted spoon and set aside.

2. Turn the heat up and add the pork shoulder and ribs. Brown the meat for a few minutes and season well. Remove from the pan and set aside with the lardons.

3. Add the chilli, onions, red pepper and garlic to the pan. Cook over a low heat for 5 minutes, then add the bay leaves, thyme, paprika and orange zest. Return all the meat to the pan and cook together for 5 minutes, then pour in the stock.

4. Bring up to the boil and simmer for about an hour, or until the pork flakes off the bone. Add the black beans, edamame, ham hock and kale. Bring back up to a simmer and cook for a few minutes, or until the kale has wilted. Season and add a little vinegar. Add extra stock to let the soup down to the required consistency.

5. To make the farofa, heat the oil in a large, heavy-based frying pan. Cook the onion for 5 minutes, then tip in the flour and season with the salt . Turn the heat down and cook the flour for about 10 minutes, stirring constantly, so the flour becomes slightly toasted and crunchy.

6. Serve the soup with a sprinkling of farofa and the tomatillo salsa from page 248, if liked.

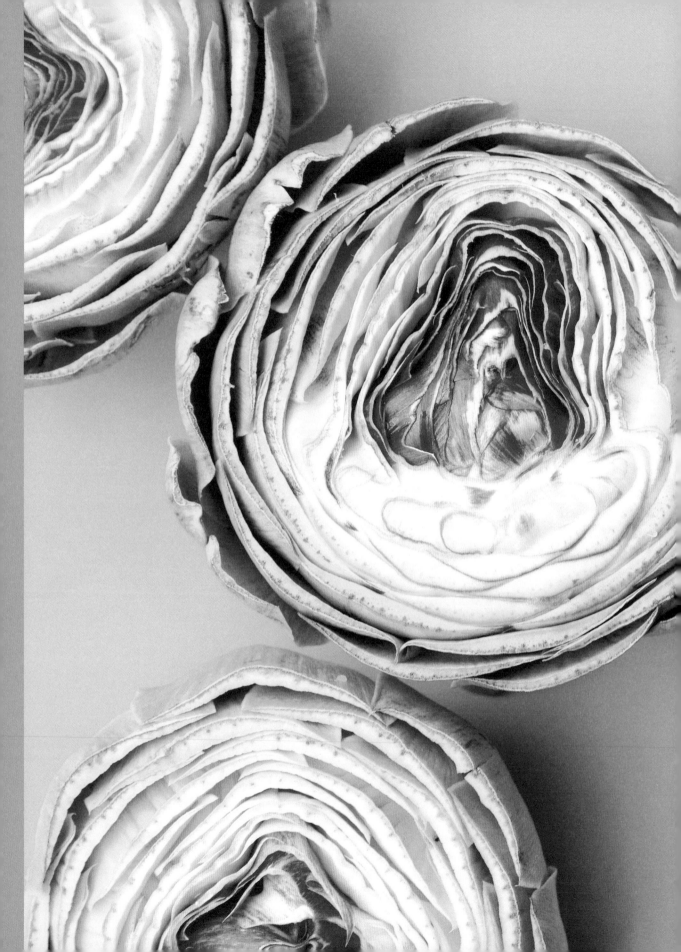

MEALS FOR A CROWD

QUICK
MIDWINTER BRISKET

In the bleak midwinter, this brisket and root vegetable medley will brighten up suppertime. If you fancy saving energy, money and time (we do), you can make this in a pressure cooker. If you're using a regular casserole dish, however, double the cooking times.

PREP TIME: 20 MINS · COOK TIME: 1 HOUR 20 MINS

about 1–2kg **brisket**

1 teaspoon **salt**

1 teaspoon **freshly ground black pepper**

1 tablespoon **olive oil**

4 large **onions**, thinly sliced

1 **bay leaf**

1 sprig of **fresh thyme**

6 cloves of **garlic**, crushed

1 tablespoon **tomato purée**

100ml **red wine**

a dash of **balsamic vinegar**

500ml **beef or chicken stock**

1 tablespoon **Dijon mustard**

1 tablespoon **wholegrain mustard**

300g **small carrots**, peeled

300g **turnips**, peeled and quartered

300g **swede**, peeled and cut into large chunks

10 **dumplings** (see page 164)

1. Trim most of the fat and connective tissue off the brisket, leaving a thin layer of fat. Rub with salt and pepper. Heat the oil in a pressure cooker until quite hot and brown the outside of the piece of meat. If the meat is too large to fit in the pan in one piece, cut it in half or thirds.

2. Remove the meat from the pan, turn down to a medium heat, and add the onions with the bay leaf and thyme. Cook for 5 minutes, then add the garlic. Stir for a minute, then add the tomato purée, wine, vinegar and stock. Bring to a simmer and return the meat to the pan. Attach the lid to the pressure cooker and cook on high pressure for about an hour.

3. Allow the cooker to cool down for 10 minutes before opening. Remove the meat from the pan and cut into thick slices across the grain. Whisk the mustards into the sauce, then return the sliced meat to the pan along with the vegetables.

4. Place the lid back on the pan and cook on low pressure for another 30 minutes. In the last 20 minutes of cooking, separately poach the dumplings (see page 164 for method). When cool enough, remove the meat, dumplings and veg from the pan to a platter and keep warm. Turn up the heat and reduce the sauce to a coating consistency. Pour over the meat before serving and add the dumplings, be careful – they're delicate!

This is great served with braised Savoy cabbage. Feel free to use whichever root vegetables you can get your hands on.

SMOKED DUCK, FIG & WALNUT SALAD

🍴④

Autumn is the fig's time to shine. They pair so well with the gamey and rich smoked duck.

PREP TIME: 15 MINS

FOR THE DRESSING

2 tablespoons **walnut oil**

1 tablespoon **mild olive oil**

1 tablespoon **balsamic vinegar**

juice of 1 **clementine**

1 teaspoon **Dijon mustard**

1 teaspoon **raw honey**

a pinch of **cayenne pepper**

salt and **freshly ground black pepper**

FOR THE SALAD

1 head of **chicory**

50g **frisée**

leaves from ¼ **head of radicchio**

a small bunch of **watercress**

50g **walnuts**, toasted and roughly chopped

4 **figs**, quartered

seeds from ½ **pomegranate**

1 **blood orange** (or **clementine**), skinned and sliced

2 **smoked duck breasts**, thinly sliced

1. Whisk all the dressing ingredients together and season well.

2. Separate the leaves from the chicory and place in a bowl with the rest of the salad leaves.

3. Toss the leaves with most of the salad dressing and place on a platter, reserving about a quarter of the dressing. Top with the rest of the salad ingredients and drizzle with the rest of the dressing to serve.

If you can't find smoked duck, you could use the confit duck recipe from page 192 or just a regular cooked duck breast.

PROSCIUTTO, PORCINI & LEEK 'LASAGNE'

Using celeriac where once was pasta adds a creamy and earthy layer to this twist on an Italian classic, *vincisgrassi*. At first blush, this recipe seems quite complicated but it's actually very simple. All the preparation can be done ahead of time, and the lasagne can be assembled and cooked just before serving.

PREP TIME: 40 MINS · COOK TIME: 1 HOUR 10 MINS

15g **dried porcini mushrooms**

250ml **boiling water**

1 **celeriac**, peeled

4 tablespoons **olive oil**

4–6 **leeks**, trimmed and halved

200g **spinach**

300g **cauliflower florets**

200ml **almond milk**

a pinch of **ground nutmeg**

1 **shallot**, finely chopped

1 clove of **garlic**, crushed

1 tablespoon **truffle oil**

2 tablespoons chopped **fresh parsley**

2 teaspoons chopped **fresh tarragon**

100g **prosciutto slices**

extra **truffle oil** for drizzling (optional)

salt and **freshly ground black pepper**

1. Heat the oven to 200°C/400°F/gas mark 6.

2. Soak the dried porcini in the boiling water.

3. Thinly slice the celeriac (think lasagne sheet thickness), then toss the sheets in 2 tablespoons of olive oil and season. Lay the celeriac on baking trays and cook in the oven for about 20 minutes, until just soft. It doesn't matter if the sheets are overlapping. Remove from the oven and set aside.

4. Cook the leeks for a few minutes in boiling salted water until tender. Remove from the pan, drain well and season.

5. Heat 1 tablespoon of olive oil in a large pan, tip in the spinach, season and cook until wilted. Tip into a colander to drain. When cool enough, squeeze out any excess moisture and chop roughly.

6. Steam the cauliflower florets until tender. Using a stick blender, blend with the almond milk until very smooth and season well with nutmeg, salt and pepper. You're making the equivalent of a béchamel here.

7. Drain the soaked porcini, reserving the soaking liquid. Chop the mushrooms finely and cook in the remaining tablespoon of olive oil with the chopped shallots for 5 minutes. Add the garlic and cook for a further minute, then tip in the soaking liquid. Bring to the boil and reduce the liquid until it has a thick coating consistency. Stir in the cauliflower purée, truffle oil and herbs. Season well.

8. To assemble the lasagne, layer up the ingredients in an ovenproof dish. First add a little of the sauce to the base of the dish and spread out with the back of a spoon. Top with celeriac pieces and slices of prosciutto. Add a single layer of leeks, cutting them to fit the dish, and sprinkle with chopped spinach. Drizzle with a little more sauce and repeat the process until all the ingredients have been used up, finishing with a layer of celeriac topped with the porcini sauce.

9. Bake in the oven for about 25 minutes, then remove and allow to stand for 10 minutes before serving. Extra truffle oil can be drizzled on when serving, if you like.

To peel a celeriac, it's best to use a serrated knife and saw around it. A vegetable peeler won't really work.

MEATLOAF

We would do anything for loaf, but we won't do that.

PREP TIME: 20 MINS · COOK TIME: I HOUR 10 MINS

25g **dried porcini mushrooms**

200ml **boiling water**

2 tablespoons **olive oil**

1 **onion**, finely chopped

2 sticks of **celery**, finely chopped

1 **carrot**, finely chopped

1 **leek**, finely chopped

1 **red pepper**, finely chopped

6 **spring onions**, chopped

2 cloves of **garlic**, crushed

500g **minced veal**

500g **minced pork**

150g **chicken livers**, trimmed

2 teaspoons **chilli sauce**

2 teaspoons **tomato purée**

100ml **almond milk**

3 **eggs**, beaten

75g **ground almonds** (or
   gluten-free breadcrumbs)

½ teaspoon **ground cumin**

½ teaspoon **ground nutmeg**

½ teaspoon **paprika**

2 teaspoons **freshly ground black
   pepper**

salt

FOR THE SCOTCH EGGS

10 **eggs**

100g **rice flour**

150g **gluten-free breadcrumbs** or
   polenta

rapeseed oil, for deep-frying

1. Heat the oven to 170°C/350°F/gas mark 3.

2. Soak the dried porcini in the boiling water. Set aside for 15 minutes.

3. Heat the oil in a large pan and cook all the finely chopped vegetables (use a food processor to get them super fine) for about 15 minutes over a low heat, making sure they do not brown or catch on the pan.

4. Drain the porcini, reserving the liquid, and chop the mushrooms finely. Add to the pan of veg with the garlic and cook for another 5 minutes. Tip the contents of the pan into a bowl and allow to cool. The porcini soaking liquor can be frozen and used in risottos or gravy.

5. Add the veal and pork to the vegetable mix. Blitz the chicken livers in a food processor for a few seconds and pour into the bowl. Add the rest of the ingredients and mix well so that everything is evenly distributed.

6. It's a good idea to fry and taste a little of the mixture, so that the seasoning can be adjusted before cooking. Once you're satisfied, spoon the mixture into a lined loaf tin and place in a bain-marie in the oven for an hour.

7. To serve, turn out on to a serving dish and slice.

 # SCOTCH EGGS

The uncooked meatloaf mixture makes the perfect casing for Scotch eggs. Scotch eggs are great. This recipe is great. It is a rather wet mixture, but this helps to maintain the moisture through cooking.

PREP TIME: I5 MINS · COOK TIME: I6 MINS

1. Boil 8 of the eggs for 5 minutes, then refresh in cold water and peel. Meanwhile, beat together the remaining eggs well.

2. Wrap the boiled eggs in a 1–2cm layer of the meatloaf mixture.

3. Roll the eggs first in rice flour, then in beaten egg and finally either gluten-free breadcrumbs or polenta.

4. Heat the oil for deep-frying to 180°C and fry the Scotch eggs for 10 minutes, until golden brown. Drain on kitchen paper before serving.

CHICKPEA TAGLIATELLE

This chickpea pasta is just the ticket for all the chic chicks in your life.
Jane made this for a gluten-free pasta night at her kitchen, and all the children loved it.

**PREP TIME: 30 MINS · SOAK TIME: OVERNIGHT · CHILL TIME: OVERNIGHT
COOK TIME: 1 HOUR 10 MINS**

200g **chickpeas**, soaked overnight

6 cloves of **garlic**, crushed

½ **leek**, finely sliced

½ **red onion**, diced

2 **cherry tomatoes**, halved

1 small **dried chilli**, finely sliced

1 sprig of **fresh rosemary**

150ml **olive oil**, for frying

salt and **freshly ground black
   pepper**

FOR THE PASTA DOUGH

300g **gram flour**

3 tablespoons **arrowroot**

a pinch of **salt**

3 **eggs**

millet flour, for rolling

1. Place the gram flour, arrowroot and salt in a food processor. Blitz and add the eggs one by one. Empty the dough on to a clean surface and knead lightly to bring it together. If the dough feels sticky, add extra gram flour. Divide the dough into 4 and wrap in clingfilm. Leave in the refrigerator for about 30 minutes.

2. Roll out each piece of dough on a surface sprinkled with a little millet flour. The dough can now be fed through a pasta machine until fairly thin. Alternatively, it can be rolled out by hand with a rolling pin. Cut the pasta sheets into strips about 1cm wide. Leave on a lightly floured tray.

3. Drain the chickpeas and put them into a pan. Cover with water and add the vegetables, chilli and rosemary. Bring to the boil, then simmer for about an hour, until the chickpeas are tender. Make sure the chickpeas are always covered with water.

4. Remove the vegetables along with 100ml of liquid and blitz together to make your sauce. Return it to the pan and stir into the chickpeas. Season well.

5. Divide the tagliatelle roughly into 3. Cook two-thirds in lots of boiling salted water. Fry the final third in hot olive oil until the pieces of pasta crisp up. Remove with a slotted spoon and drain on kitchen paper.

6. Combine the cooked pasta with the chickpeas, adding a little extra water so the pasta isn't dry. Season well and add the fried crisp pasta pieces before serving.

PIGEON & SQUASH SALAD

Pigeons are gamey birds, with a deep nutty flavour. Remember, you want a wood pigeon, not a Trafalgar Square pigeon. If you can't source it, partridge, guinea fowl or pheasant would also be delicious. This is a meal fit for a proper autumn afternoon.

PREP TIME: 20 MINS · COOK TIME: 50 MINS

300g **beetroot**

5 tablespoons **olive oil**

300g **butternut squash**, peeled and cut into 1cm slices

8 **pigeon breasts**

8 slices of **prosciutto**

1 tablespoon **walnut oil**

1 tablespoon **pumpkin seed oil**

1 tablespoon **sherry vinegar**

100g **mixed baby leaves**

50g **toasted walnuts**

2 tablespoons **toasted pumpkin seeds**

salt and **freshly ground black pepper**

1. Heat the oven to 180°C/350°F/gas mark 4.

2. Peel the beetroot and cut into fine dice. Toss with 2 tablespoons of olive oil and season. Place on a baking tray and cover with foil. Bake for about 40 minutes, or until tender.

3. After the beetroot has been in for 10 minutes, toss the squash in 1 tablespoon of olive oil and season well. Place on a baking tray and roast for about 30 minutes, or until tender. Allow both vegetables to cool. This way, both your vegetables will be out of the oven at the same time.

4. Season the pigeon breasts and heat 1 tablespoon of oil in a large non-stick frying pan. Cook the pigeon for about 2 minutes on each side, then leave to rest. Fry the prosciutto slices for a minute to crisp up, and set aside with the pigeon.

5. Whisk the walnut oil, pumpkin seed oil and the remaining tablespoon of olive oil with the sherry vinegar and season well. Toss the leaves in half the dressing and arrange on a plate with the beetroot and squash.

6. Slice the pigeon and arrange on top of the salad with the prosciutto. Sprinkle with the seeds and nuts. Drizzle with the rest of the dressing to serve.

BEEF SHIN & VEGETABLE SOUP

The initial cooking of the beef can be done in a pressure cooker to cut down the cooking time. The vegetables given are only a suggestion – this is a good soup for using up all those leftover veggies that accumulate at the bottom of your refrigerator and leave you a little stumped.

PREP TIME: 20 MINS · COOK TIME: 2 HOURS 10 MINS

1 tablespoon **rice bran oil**

800g **shin of beef on the bone**, cut into 4 pieces

2 **onions**, sliced

1 × 3cm cube of **ginger**, sliced

6 cloves of **garlic**, sliced

2 **red chillies**, sliced

2 **star anise**

1 tablespoon **tamari**

1.2 litres **beef** or **chicken stock**

100g **rice noodles** (or **soba**)

100g **purple sprouting broccoli**, trimmed

100g **carrots** and/or **turnips**, cut into thin batons

50g **mushrooms**, sliced

100g **pak choi** or **other greens**

1 tablespoon chopped **fresh coriander**, to serve

1 tablespoon chopped **fresh chives**, to serve

1. Heat the oil in a large pan and brown the pieces of beef. Remove from the pan, then turn down the heat and add the onions, ginger, garlic and chillies. Cook for a minute, then add the star anise, tamari and stock. Bring to a simmer and return the beef to the pan. Cover and cook over a low heat for 2 hours, or until the beef is tender.

2. In a separate pan, cover the noodles with boiling water and leave for 10 minutes. Drain well.

3. Add the vegetables to the soup – adding extra stock if required. Cook for another 5 minutes. Take off the heat and add the rice noodles. Serve sprinkled with the herbs.

STUFFED SQUID

These squid are full of a fennel and chard stuffing, and will even convert fennel haters. When you're stuffing them, don't over-fill, because the squid will shrink once it's cooked.

PREP TIME: 30 MINS · COOK TIME: 30 MINS

32 **small squid**, cleaned

4 tablespoons **olive oil**

4 cloves of **garlic**, crushed

500g good **tomatoes**, skinned and chopped

2 bunches of **fresh basil**, shredded

extra virgin olive oil, for drizzling

FOR THE STUFFING

2 tablespoons **olive oil**

2 **shallots**, finely chopped

1 head of **fennel**, finely chopped

2 teaspoons **ground fennel seeds**

1 teaspoon **chilli flakes**

2 cloves of **garlic**, chopped

4 **anchovies**, chopped

100g **rainbow chard**, cooked

100g **ground almonds**

salt and **freshly ground black pepper**

1. Heat the olive oil for the stuffing in a large pan. Add the shallots and fennel and cook for 10 minutes, or until tender. Stir in the ground fennel seeds, chilli flakes and garlic and cook for a minute. Tip in the anchovies, then remove from the heat and stir until the anchovies dissolve.

2. Squeeze any excess moisture out of the chard and chop finely. Add to the pan and cook for a minute. Season well. Remove from the heat and stir in the almonds. Allow to cool.

3. Stuff each squid with the fennel and chard stuffing. Tuck the tentacles of each squid back into the opening of its squid tube and secure with a small cocktail stick.

4. Heat the olive oil in a large non-stick frying pan. Add all the squid and cook over a high heat to brown for 2 minutes. Remove from the pan with a slotted spoon.

5. Add the garlic to the pan and stir for a minute. Tip in the tomatoes and cook for 5 minutes over a medium heat. Stir in the basil and return the squid to the pan. Cook over a low heat for 10 minutes. Season well and drizzle with good extra virgin olive oil to serve.

These are brilliant served with a large glass of white wine (or, as Jane calls it, lady petrol).

POTATO GNOCCHI

Knock, knock, gnocchi on heaven's door.
You need floury potatoes for this recipe, like King Edward or Desiree.

PREP TIME: 10 MINS · COOK TIME: 50 MINS

500g **potatoes**

4 tablespoons **potato starch**

4 tablespoons **arrowroot**

2 teaspoons **cornflour**

salt

1. Heat the oven to 180°C/350°F/gas mark 4.

2. Place the potatoes on the rack of the oven and bake for about 45 minutes, or until cooked through. The time will depend on the size of the potatoes. When you take them out of the oven, cut each potato in half to release steam and let the moisture evaporate.

3. Sieve together all the dry ingredients and mix well. Sprinkle about a quarter of the flour mixture on to a clean dry surface. (You will probably not need to use all of this mixture, but it really depends on the starch content of your potatoes.)

4. Bring lots of salted water to the boil.

5. While the potatoes are still hot, scoop out the flesh into a potato ricer and rice the potatoes directly on to the floured surface. Sprinkle with more flour mixture (but hold a bit back).

6. Bring the dough together with your hands and knead briefly. It should be soft, but manageable. Pinch off a small piece of the dough and drop it into the boiling water as a tester. If it falls apart add more flour mixture. If not, you're good to go. Roll the dough into long logs and cut into pieces about 1cm wide. Press the top of each piece with the tines of a fork and dust with the remaining flour mixture, this texture helps the gnocchi to take on the flavour of whatever sauce you use with it.

7. Simmer for a few minutes, until all the gnocchi have come to the surface. Remove with a slotted spoon on to a plate. The gnocchi can be used straight away, with a sauce, or refrigerated and fried in olive oil later.

We served this with 1 tablespoon of truffle paste mixed with a few tablespoons of cashew cream (see page 270, but leave out the vanilla and honey) and a little of the pasta water.

TORTILLA SOUP

Poaching a chicken in stock will give you enough meat for the soup and loads of well-flavoured stock for the base.

PREP TIME: 15 MINS · COOK TIME: 1 HOUR

6 **corn tortillas**

4 tablespoons **olive oil**

6 **red chillies**

1 litre **chicken stock**

kernels from 2 **sweetcorn cobs**, or 1 × 400g tins of **sweetcorn**, drained

1 **onion**, finely chopped

2 cloves of **garlic**, crushed

1 sprig of **fresh thyme**

1 teaspoon **ground cumin**

1 teaspoon **smoked paprika**

½ teaspoon **ground cinnamon**

1 × 400g tin of **tomatoes**

1 **cooked chicken** (meat removed from carcass) or 4 cooked **chicken breasts**, shredded

2 teaspoons **raw honey**

300g **rainbow chard**, stems removed and leaves shredded

juice of 1 **lime**

2 **avocados**, chopped

fresh coriander, chopped

salt and **freshly ground black pepper**

1. Heat the oven to 180°C/350°F/gas mark 4.

2. Cut the tortillas into 1cm wide strips. Toss them in half the olive oil and bake in the oven for about 10 minutes, or until golden and crisp. Set aside.

3. Chop 4 of the chillies, removing the seeds, then put them into a pan with the chicken stock, bring to the boil, and simmer for 15 minutes. Slice the remaining 2 chillies.

4. Cook the corn kernels in the remaining oil in a frying pan over a high heat until they are slightly browned. Add the onion, sliced chillies, garlic and thyme. Cook for 5 minutes, then add the spices and stir well. Add the tomatoes, including the juice from the tin, and bring to a simmer. Cook for about 20 minutes over a low heat.

5. Blend the chicken stock with the large chillies, using a stick blender, and add to the tomato sauce. Return to a simmer and add the shredded chicken, honey and chard. Cook for another 10 minutes, adding more stock if required.

6. Finish with a good squeeze of lime juice and check the seasoning.

7. To serve, divide half the tortilla pieces between 6 bowls. Ladle the soup over the top and finish with the rest of the tortilla strips, avocado and fresh coriander.

SPICED CHICKEN LIVER SALAD
WITH MUSTARD SEED VINAIGRETTE

A zingy, summer dinner party masterpiece.

PREP TIME: 15 MINS · COOK TIME: 10 MINS

400g **chicken livers**

2 tablespoons **garam masala**

2 tablespoons **rice bran oil**

150g **French beans**, trimmed

50g **frisée**

100g **cherry tomatoes**, halved

1 head of **chicory**

100g **cooked Puy lentils**

1 **globe artichoke**, prepped and
   cooked or 100g **deli artichokes**,
   halved

FOR THE DRESSING

1 tablespoon **olive oil**

2 tablespoons **mustard seeds**

1 **shallot**, finely chopped

2 tablespoons **cider vinegar**

1 tablespoon **Dijon mustard**

1 teaspoon **maple syrup**

3 tablespoons **rapeseed oil**

salt and **freshly ground black
   pepper**

1. To make the dressing heat the olive oil in a small frying pan and add the mustard seeds. When the seeds start to pop, cover the pan and take off the heat. Whisk together the rest of the dressing ingredients until you have an emulsion. Season and add the mustard seeds.

2. Trim the chicken livers and toss with the garam masala. Heat the rice bran oil in a large non-stick pan and fry the chicken livers for 2–3 minutes, until they are lightly browned and pink in the middle. Set aside.

3. Cook the French beans in lots of boiling salted water for 3 minutes. Drain and refresh in cold water.

4. Toss the beans, frisée, tomatoes and chicory with a little of the dressing. Arrange on a plate and sprinkle with the cooked lentils and artichokes. Top with the chicken livers and any juices that have gathered in the pan. Drizzle with more dressing to serve.

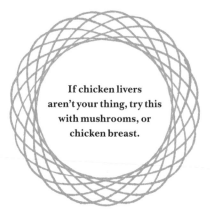

If chicken livers
aren't your thing, try this
with mushrooms, or
chicken breast.

CONFIT DUCK

Confit duck has so many uses, and makes you feel like you've just graduated from Le Cordon Bleu. It keeps for up to two weeks preserved in its fat (which is great for roasting veg with), and can be taken out, crisped up quickly and used in all the variations we've come up with here. If you can't find a jar of duck fat, heat the duck trimmings long and slow in a low oven to render the fat. Or just use oil instead.

**PREP TIME: 10 MINS · SALT TIME: OVERNIGHT
COOK TIME: 2 HOURS 15 MINS**

6 **duck legs**

50g **rock salt**

1 tablespoon **black peppercorns**, crushed

6 cloves of **garlic**, sliced

5 sprigs of **fresh thyme**

3 **bay leaves**

750g **duck fat**

1. Dry the duck legs. Mix together the salt, pepper, garlic, thyme and bay leaves. Sprinkle one-third of the mix on to a tray or dish into which all the duck legs will fit snugly. Put the duck legs in, skin side down, and sprinkle with the rest of the salt mix. Cover and leave in the refrigerator overnight, or for at least 12 hours.

2. Heat the oven to 120°C/250°F/gas mark ½.

3. Take the duck legs out of the cure and rub off any excess salt. Pat dry with kitchen paper and place in a baking dish, skin side up. Add some of the sliced garlic, thyme and bay leaves from the cure. Spoon over the duck fat and cover the tray with a lid or foil. Cook in a low oven for about 2 hours, or until the meat is tender. Allow to cool in the fat.

4. Keep the duck legs and fat in the refrigerator, where they will keep up to 2 weeks.

5. To cook, remove the legs from the fat, scraping off any excess. Heat an ovenproof frying pan and put the legs in, skin side down. Cook for 2 minutes, then flip over and place in a hot oven for 5–10 minutes, until the skin is crisp and brown. Serve with one of the accompaniments overleaf.

3.

2.

1.

1. CASSOULET

PREP TIME: 15 MINS · COOK TIME: 40 MINS

1 tablespoon **duck fat**

200g **gluten-free pork sausages**, cut into chunks

1 **onion**, chopped

1 **carrot**, chopped

1 stick of **celery**, chopped

3 cloves of **garlic**, crushed

2 teaspoons **fennel seeds**, crushed

a pinch of **dried chilli flakes**

2 teaspoons chopped **fresh rosemary**

½ × 400g tin of **chopped tomatoes**

1 × 400g tin of **cannellini beans**, drained and rinsed

150ml **chicken stock**

1 tablespoon chopped **fresh parsley**

salt and **freshly ground black pepper**

1. Heat the duck fat in a large frying pan. Brown the sausages and remove from the pan.

2. Add the vegetables and cook over a low heat for 15 minutes without browning. Add the garlic, fennel seeds, chilli flakes and rosemary. Cook for a minute, then tip in the chopped tomatoes and the sausages.

3. Simmer for 10 minutes, then add the beans and stock. Cook for another 10 minutes, then check the seasoning and serve with the duck, sprinkled with parsley.

2. MIDDLE EASTERN SLAW

PREP TIME: 10 MINS

1 large **carrot**, grated

1 **red onion**, finely chopped

1 clove of **garlic**, crushed

1 **red chilli**, chopped

¼ small **red cabbage**, finely shredded

1 **kohlrabi**, grated

1 tablespoon chopped **fresh parsley**

1 tablespoon chopped **fresh mint**

1 **orange**, skin and pith removed, chopped

1 teaspoon **pomegranate molasses**

2 tablespoons **pine nuts**, toasted

2 tablespoons **olive oil**

1 tablespoon **balsamic vinegar**

salt and **freshly ground black pepper**

1. Toss all the ingredients together.

2. Season well. This is great served with the duck (but is also veggie on its own).

These accompaniments all serve 6 people.

3. DUCK RAGÙ

The duck ragù recipe comes from Ed at the Curator Kitchen in Totnes – who normally serves it with pappardelle. He cooks the sauce for hours, but we have tried to cut down the cooking time here. We'd recommend this sauce with our celeriac or chickpea pastas (see pages 158 and 178).

PREP TIME: 30 MINS · COOK TIME: I HOUR 30 MINS

250g **gluten-free pasta** of choice

½ **Savoy cabbage**, shredded

1 tablespoon **olive oil**

3 tablespoons chopped **fresh parsley**

salt and **freshly ground black pepper**

FOR THE RAGÙ

2 tablespoons **olive oil**

2 tablespoons **duck fat**

1 **onion**, chopped

2 sticks of **celery**, chopped

1 **leek**, chopped

2 **carrots**, chopped

1 **bay leaf**

2 **cloves**

1 × 2cm stick of **cinnamon**

1 **star anise**

2 strips of **orange zest**

4 cloves of **garlic**, crushed

1 × 400g tin of **chopped tomatoes**

4 **cooked duck legs**

250ml **red wine**

200ml **chicken or duck stock**

salt and **freshly ground black pepper**

1. Heat the oil and duck fat for the ragù in a large pan. Add the chopped vegetables, bay leaf, spices and orange zest, and cook for about 30 minutes over a low heat. Add the garlic and cook for another minute, then tip in the tomatoes and simmer for another 15 minutes.

2. Take the meat off the duck legs and chop into large chunks. Reserve the meat, then add the wine, bones and stock to the pan. Bring to the boil and simmer until the sauce has thickened. Remove the bones, spices and orange zest, then take out half the sauce and blend the rest with a stick blender until smooth. Put the unblended sauce back into the pan and mix with the smooth sauce.

3. Add the duck pieces to the sauce and simmer for about another 30 minutes, or longer if you have the time. If it gets too dry at any stage, add more chicken stock or boiling water. Season well.

4. Cook the pasta in lots of boiling water according to the instructions. Add the cabbage to the pan 2 minutes before the pasta is ready. Drain well, season and toss with a little olive oil.

5. Toss the pasta and cabbage with the duck sauce, and serve sprinkled with lots of chopped parsley.

LEON LAMB & RHUBARB KORESH

A fresh, clean and complex spring stew. Complex tasting, not making. We've suggested using lamb shoulder here, but you could use lamb mince too.

PREP TIME: 15 MINS · COOK TIME: 1 HOUR 45 MINS

2 **onions**, peeled and chopped

2 tablespoons **olive oil**

750g **lamb shoulder**, diced

1 teaspoon **ground turmeric**

300ml **chicken stock**

1 bunch of **fresh flat-leaf parsley**, finely chopped

1 bunch of **fresh mint**, finely chopped

1 bunch of **fresh coriander**, finely chopped

a small pinch of **saffron**, soaked in 2 tablespoons **hot water**

juice of 1 **lime**

500g **rhubarb**, cut into bite-size pieces

coconut sugar, to taste

extra herbs, chopped, to finish

salt and **freshly ground black pepper**

1. In a casserole dish, soften the onions in half the olive oil for 5 minutes, then remove and set aside.

2. Brown the meat over a high heat in batches. You may need to add a little more oil. When all the meat is browned, return the onions to the pan and season with salt, pepper and turmeric. Add the stock, or enough just to cover. Bring to the boil, then turn the heat down to a simmer, cover and cook for about 1 hour on a low heat.

3. Meanwhile, in a frying pan, heat the remaining oil and fry the parsley, mint and coriander, stirring all the time, for about 7–10 minutes. This concentrates their flavours and gives them texture.

4. Add the fried herbs, saffron and lime juice to the lamb after it has cooked for an hour. Bring back to a simmer and cook for 5–10 minutes.

5. Now add the rhubarb, and simmer for another 10–15 minutes.

6. Taste for seasoning – you may want to add a touch of coconut sugar at this point. Serve sprinkled with extra herbs.

MEALS FOR A CROWD

TOFU ADOBO

Cooking meat with vinegar is the traditional 'adobo' method of cooking in the Philippines. We've swapped the meat for tofu, and it's so good you'll want a double portion.

PREP TIME: 10 MINS · COOK TIME: 50 MINS

600g **extra firm tofu**

5 cloves of **garlic**, sliced

1 tablespoon **rice bran oil**

500ml **vegetable stock**

50ml **tamari**

50ml **coconut vinegar**

3 teaspoons **coarsely ground black peppercorns**

3 **bay leaves**

150g **French beans**, trimmed

1 teaspoon **coconut sugar**

1 teaspoon **cornflour**

2 **spring onions**, chopped

1. Heat the oven to 220°C/425°F/gas mark 7.

2. Slice the tofu about 1cm thick and cut each piece in half. Leave on kitchen paper to absorb the excess water for about an hour. Place on a sheet of baking parchment on a baking tray and roast in the hot oven for about 30 minutes, turning it over halfway so the tofu is browned all over.

3. While the tofu is browning, heat a large pan and cook the garlic in the oil for a minute. Add the stock, tamari, vinegar, pepper and bay leaves. Bring to the boil, then simmer for about 20 minutes, until the sauce has reduced slightly and thickened.

4. Add the beans, sugar and browned tofu and simmer for another 5 minutes. Mix the cornflour with a little water and stir into the sauce. Cook for another minute to thicken the mixture. Serve sprinkled with chopped spring onion with cauliflower rice on the side, if liked.

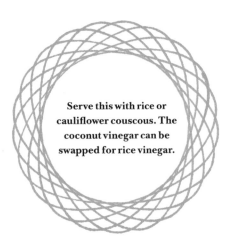

Serve this with rice or cauliflower couscous. The coconut vinegar can be swapped for rice vinegar.

ROASTED VEGETABLE MOLE

🍴④🍴

The vegetables given below are suggestions – any combination would work well with the rich, dark mole sauce. This sauce is a labour of love, and the praise you will receive will be totally worth it. Any leftover sauce is worth freezing for a later date.

PREP TIME: 30 MINS · SOAK TIME: 30 MINS · COOK TIME: 50 MINS

FOR THE MOLE

25g **dried ancho chillies**

2 large **tomatoes**, skinned

a pinch of **dried oregano**

1 tablespoon **sesame seeds**

1 tablespoon **pumpkin seeds**

1 tablespoon **walnuts**

a pinch of **ground cinnamon**

½ teaspoon **ground cumin**

½ teaspoon **fennel seeds**

3 **cloves**

6 **black peppercorns**

1 **onion**, chopped

3 tablespoons **olive oil**

2 teaspoons **smoked paprika**

70g **raisins**

50g **flaked almonds**

vegetable stock, if needed

50g **sugar-free dark chocolate**

salt and **freshly ground black pepper**

FOR THE VEGETABLES

400g **butternut squash**

1 **cauliflower**

2 **red onions**

1 **red pepper**

kernels from 2 **cobs of corn**

2 tablespoons **olive oil**

salt and **freshly ground black pepper**

1. Heat the oven to 200°C/400°F/gas mark 6.

2. Pour boiling water over the ancho chillies until they're just covered, and leave for at least 30 minutes.

3. Roughly chop the tomatoes and place them in a large bowl with the oregano. Lightly toast the seeds and nuts until golden brown, and add to the tomatoes.

4. Lightly toast the cinnamon, cumin, fennel seeds, cloves and peppercorns until fragrant, then grind in a spice grinder, or in a pestle and mortar. Add to the bowl.

5. In a large frying pan, cook the onion in the olive oil for 10 minutes over a medium heat. Add the smoked paprika, raisins and almonds. Continue to cook for 10 minutes, until the raisins have puffed up and the almonds are lightly toasted.

6. Drain the ancho chillies and discard the stalks, reserving the soaking liquid. Slice the chillies thinly and add to the pan along with the tomato and seed mix. Stir well and cook for 10 minutes. Pour in about 200ml of the chilli soaking liquid or veg stock and bring to a simmer. Cook for 10 more minutes, or until you have a thick sauce.

7. Grate the chocolate into the sauce. Season well with salt and tip into a food processor or liquidizer. Blitz until smooth. At this point the sauce can be sieved for a smooth finish, but you may prefer a bit of texture.

8. Cut the squash into 2cm chunks. Separate the cauliflower into smaller florets. Cut the onions and pepper into wedges. Toss all the vegetables in a bowl with the corn and olive oil. Season well and spoon on to a baking tray. Cook in the oven for about 25 minutes.

9. Serve the roasted veg topped with the mole sauce.

This sauce would also go well with sweet potato quesadillas (see page 28). When in season, swap half the cauliflower for romanesco.

CRAB SALAD
WITH COURCHAMPS SAUCE

We love Courchamps sauce because it uses the brown meat of the crab which often goes to waste.

PREP TIME: 20 MINS

50g **rocket**

1 head of **fennel**, shaved

150g **asparagus spears**, cooked
   and cut into thin slices

1 tablespoon **lemon juice**

1 tablespoon **olive oil**

300g **white crabmeat**

handful of **cress**, to serve

FOR THE SAUCE

200g **brown crabmeat**

3 **shallots**, finely chopped

3 tablespoons chopped **fresh
   tarragon**

3 tablespoons chopped **fresh
   parsley**

2 teaspoons **Dijon mustard**

1 teaspoon **tamari**

2 tablespoons **Sambuca**, or other
   aniseed liqueur

juice of ½ **lemon**

50ml **olive oil**

salt and **freshly ground black
   pepper**

1. Blitz together all the sauce ingredients until smooth. Season well.

2. Toss the rocket with the fennel, asparagus, lemon and oil. Top with the white crabmeat and drizzle with the Courchamps sauce. Scatter with cress to serve.

LAMB, FIG & WALNUT TAGINE

Once you make this, you'll never fig-etabout it. One to eat near a fire, in the dead of winter.

PREP TIME: 15 MINS · COOK TIME: 2 HOURS 30 MINS

800g **lamb shoulder**, cut into
    2cm dice

3 tablespoons **sunflower oil**

3 **onions** (**red** or **white**), each
    sliced into 4 large discs

1½ teaspoons **ground ginger**

2 teaspoons **ground cinnamon**

1 teaspoon **whole coriander
    seeds**, coarsely ground

2 teaspoons **ground cumin**

4 strips of **orange peel**

1 stick of **cinnamon**

2 teaspoons **raw honey**

500ml **lamb** or **chicken stock**

12 **semi-dried figs**

16 **walnut halves**

salt and **freshly ground black
    pepper**

TO SERVE

fresh coriander leaves

extra walnuts, crushed

a drizzle of **raw honey** (optional)

1. Heat the oven to 160°C/325°F/gas mark 3.

2. Season the lamb with salt and black pepper. Heat the oil in a large casserole over medium heat and brown the meat all over. Remove the lamb and set aside. Wipe out the casserole if needed.

3. Place the onion slices across the bottom of the casserole and put the meat on top. Sprinkle all the ground spices over. Pop the orange peel and the cinnamon stick around the lamb. Drizzle with the honey.

4. Pour in about 500ml stock: you want to add enough liquid to come about a third of the way up the meat. Bring to a simmer on the hob, cover, then put into the oven and cook slowly for 2 hours. Add the figs and walnuts and cook for another 20–30 minutes.

5. Remove from the oven and serve with coriander leaves and crushed walnuts scattered over, and with a drizzle of honey, if using.

RABBIT & PRUNES

Roger this rabbit recipe immediately – Rabbit is an underrated lean and healthy meat. A true taste of autumn. Ask your butcher to joint your rabbit for you and cut it into chunks.

PREP TIME: 15 MINS · SOAK TIME: 30 MINS · COOK TIME: 1 HOUR 50 MINS

12 **prunes**

50ml **brandy**

2 tablespoons **olive oil**

2 **rabbits**, jointed

100g **bacon lardons**

1 **leek**, finely chopped

1 stick of **celery**, finely chopped

15 small **shallots** or baby onions

1 sprig of **thyme**

1 **bay leaf**

200ml **red wine**

500ml **chicken stock**

1 tablespoon **Dijon mustard**

2 teaspoons **arrowroot** (optional)

2 tablespoons chopped **fresh parsley**

salt and **freshly ground black pepper**

1. Soak the prunes in the brandy for at least 30 minutes.

2. Heat the oil in a large pan, then brown the rabbit pieces all over and remove from the pan. Add the bacon, leek and celery, and cook over a low heat for 10 minutes.

3. Add the shallots and herbs with the red wine. Bring to the boil, scraping the bottom of the pan with a wooden spoon. Add the stock and mustard, plus the prunes and any soaking liquid. Return the rabbit pieces to the pan and cover. Simmer for about 1 hour 30 minutes, or until the rabbit is tender.

4. If your sauce is not looking thick enough, mix the arrowroot with a few tablespoons of water until smooth. Add to the rabbit sauce and stir to blend. Cook for a few minutes, until the sauce has thickened. Season, and serve sprinkled with chopped parsley.

✓ / NF / SF

PORK, APPLE & CHILLI

We're not telling any porkies – this slow-cooked stew will knock your socks off.

PREP TIME: 10 MINS · COOK TIME: 1 HOUR 50 MINS

4 tablespoons **rapeseed oil**

1 **onion**, finely chopped

3 cloves of **garlic**, crushed

1kg **stewing pork** (**leg** or **shoulder**), cut into 2 cm cubes

1 **bay leaf**

3–4 sprigs of **thyme**

1–2 sprigs of **rosemary**

2 **apples** (**Cox's or Braeburns**), peeled, cored and sliced

1 **hot red chilli**, deseeded and sliced

about 425ml **cider**

200ml **chicken stock**

salt and **freshly ground black pepper**

1. Heat the oven to 180°C/350°F/gas mark 4.

2. Heat 2 tablespoons of oil in a non-stick frying pan, and gently cook the onion until it's soft and translucent. Add the garlic and cook for a further minute or so, until really fragrant.

3. Remove the onion and garlic to a casserole, then add another tablespoon of oil and, when it's hot, brown the pork in batches, adding it to the casserole as you go along with the herbs, salt and pepper.

4. When you've finished browning the pork, add the final tablespoon of oil to the frying pan if necessary, and brown the apples for about 5 minutes. About halfway through, add the chilli, stirring it through the apples, and add them both to the casserole.

5. Deglaze the frying pan with 100ml of the cider and add the stock. Bring the combined liquids to the boil. Pour this over the pork and apple and top up the casserole with the remaining cider until everything is just covered with liquid. Cover, and cook in the oven for 90 minutes.

6. Remove from the oven and use a slotted spoon to scoop out the meat and apples on to a warm plate. Bring the sauce to the boil and reduce by about a third, or until the sauce has thickened and coats the back of a spoon. Return the meat and apples to the casserole, stir through, and serve.

BIRYANI

50g **cashews**, soaked in plenty of **cold water** for 4 hours

50g **raisins**, soaked in **hot water** for at least 30 minutes

a pinch of **saffron**, soaked in 2 tablespoons **hot almond milk** for at least 30 minutes

1 head of **cauliflower**

1 tablespoon **coconut oil**

1 teaspoon **cumin seeds**

4 **cardamom pods**, bruised

3 **cloves**

1 **star anise**

1 **bay leaf**

1 × 2cm stick of **cinnamon**

a pinch of **ground mace**

2 cloves of **garlic**, crushed

1 × 2cm piece of **ginger**, grated

½ teaspoon **ground turmeric**

a large pinch of **dried chilli flakes**

1 teaspoon **garam masala**

2 **parsnips**, peeled and cut into small chunks

200g **butternut squash**, peeled and cut into small chunks

100g **French beans**, trimmed and cut into 2–3cm lengths

10 **radishes**, halved

100g **mushrooms**, cut into quarters

200g **cooked chickpeas**

100g **cooked spinach**, chopped

salt and freshly ground **black pepper**

1 tablespoon each chopped **fresh coriander** and **mint**, to serve

The ingredient list looks very long here, but it's mainly the array of spices used to make the dish fragrant. A good-quality curry paste could be used instead. Feel free to substitute the vegetables for whatever you have on hand.

PREP TIME: 30 MINS · SOAK TIME: 4 HOURS COOK TIME: 30 MINS

1. Blitz the cauliflower florets into tiny pieces in a food processor, or use a grater, and set aside.

2. Heat the oil over a gentle heat in a large pan and add the cumin seeds, cardamom pods, cloves, star anise, bay leaf, cinnamon and mace. Cook for a few minutes. Add the garlic and ginger, along with the turmeric, chilli flakes and garam masala and cook for another minute.

3. Tip in the parsnips and squash. Stir well and cover. Allow to cook for 10 minutes, then add the beans, radishes and mushrooms. Cover and cook for another 5 minutes.

4. Add the chickpeas and spinach, along with the blitzed cauliflower rice and the drained cashew nuts. Turn up the heat and cook for 5 minutes, stirring well to prevent sticking.

5. Drain the raisins and squeeze out any excess moisture. Add to the cauliflower rice mixture along with the saffron milk. Season well and fold through. Cover and leave for 10 minutes.

6. Serve with lots of chopped coriander and mint.

Arti, a splendid LEON accountant, makes her biryani with chopped oven chips (yes) as a week-night shortcut, with sweetcorn, chopped tomatoes, peppers and pomegranate seeds.

GRILLED OCTOPUS SALAD

The potato salad served with the octopus is fab on its own or as an accompaniment to any summer lunch.

PREP TIME: 20 MINS · COOK TIME: 1 HOUR 30 MINS

1kg **octopus**, cleaned

2 tablespoons **olive oil**

2 **red chillies**

10 cloves of **garlic**, 8 peeled and left whole, 2 crushed

4 sprigs of **fresh flat-leaf parsley**

500g **new potatoes**

3 **red onions**, finely chopped

3 tablespoons **cider vinegar**

2 teaspoons **coconut sugar**

150g **sugar snap peas**, trimmed and thinly sliced

150g **broad beans**, cooked

100g **peas**, cooked

2 tablespoons **extra virgin olive oil**

3 tablespoons chopped **fresh chives**

75g **pea shoots**

salt and **freshly ground black pepper**

1. Ask your fishmonger to prepare and clean the octopus tentacles and head for you. Wash well under cold running water.

2. Heat 1 tablespoon of olive oil in a pan or pressure cooker until very hot. Add the chillies, whole garlic cloves and parsley, along with the cleaned octopus. Stir for a minute and cover the pan tightly. If using a pressure cooker, cook for about 40 minutes, if not, cook over a low heat for about 1 hour, or until the octopus flesh is tender. Allow to cool in the cooking juices.

3. Cook the new potatoes in lots of boiling salted water, then drain and leave until cool enough to handle. Meanwhile, cook the onions in the remaining tablespoon of olive oil for 20 minutes, until the onions are soft. Add the crushed garlic, vinegar and sugar and mix well. Turn up the heat and reduce the liquid to a syrup.

4. Slice the potatoes when they are cool enough to handle and fold into the onions. Add the sugar snaps, broad beans and peas. Drizzle with the extra virgin olive oil and fold together. Season well, sprinkle with the chives and spoon on to a serving dish with the pea shoots.

5. Separate the tentacles of the octopus and slice the head into strips. Heat a griddle plate or barbecue until very hot, and sear the octopus pieces until charred on both sides. Place on top of the salad and season to serve.

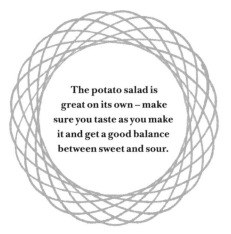

The potato salad is great on its own – make sure you taste as you make it and get a good balance between sweet and sour.

JAMAICAN CURRY

6

To achieve an authentic taste, you should use Scotch bonnet chillies, but they can be very fiery. Leaving them whole in the curry for a limited time will give a milder result.

PREP TIME: 20 MINS · MARINATING TIME: OVERNIGHT · COOK TIME: 2 HOURS

1.5kg **goat** or **lamb**, on the bone, cut into 2–3cm pieces

juice of 1 **lime**

2 teaspoons **fresh thyme leaves**

1 teaspoon **salt**

2 tablespoons **coconut oil**

2 teaspoons **coconut sugar**

2 **onions**, chopped

1 **red pepper**, chopped

1–2 **Scotch bonnet chillies**

3 cloves of **garlic**, crushed

1 × 2cm piece of **ginger**, grated

3 tablespoons **Jamaican curry powder**

5 **allspice berries**

½ × 400g tin of **chopped tomatoes**

500ml **chicken stock**

3 **sweet potatoes**, peeled and cut into 2cm chunks

1 teaspoon **cider vinegar**

salt and **freshly ground black pepper**

1. Toss the goat pieces with the lime juice, thyme leaves and salt, and leave to marinate for a few hours or overnight. Drain and pat dry with kitchen paper before cooking.

2. Heat the oil in a large pan and add the goat pieces. Sprinkle with the sugar and stir-fry for a few minutes, to brown. Remove from the pan and turn down the heat. Add the onions, red pepper, chillies, garlic and ginger. Cook for 5 minutes, then add the curry powder and allspice berries. Stir well to combine, then tip in the tomatoes.

3. Turn up the heat and return the goat to the pan with the chicken stock. Cover and simmer for about 1 hour. Add the sweet potatoes and cook for a further 40 minutes, or until the potatoes are tender. Season well and add a little vinegar before serving.

We served ours with an avocado salsa (made of chopped avocado, lime juice and coriander, seasoned with salt and pepper) – a great yoghurt alternative when the curry gets too hot.

GRILLED SARDINES WITH
AN OLIVE & CAPER STUFFING

The almond, caper and olive stuffing would also work well with chicken or squid.

PREP TIME: 20 MINS · COOK TIME: 15 MINS

8 **sardines**, trimmed and
   butterflied

1 teaspoon **olive oil**

½ **lemon**

50g **rocket**

50g **piquillo peppers**

1 head of **fennel**, shaved

1 **lemon**, cut into wedges

FOR THE STUFFING

2 tablespoons **sultanas**

50ml **olive oil**

75g **ground almonds**

1 clove of **garlic**, crushed

30g **pine nuts**, toasted

15 **black olives**, roughly chopped

3 **anchovy fillets**, chopped

2 tablespoons **capers**

3 tablespoons chopped **fresh
   parsley**

salt and **freshly ground black
   pepper**

1. To make the stuffing, soak the sultanas in very hot water. Heat the oil in a large non-stick frying pan and toast the almonds with the garlic until lightly browned, stirring well so they are evenly toasted and being careful not to burn the garlic.

2. Drain the sultanas and add to the almonds along with the pine nuts, olives, anchovies and capers. Stir and cook for a few minutes over a low heat. Remove from the heat and add the parsley. Season well.

3. Heat a griddle pan or grill until very hot. Brush the sardine skins with a little oil and season well. Place on the griddle or grill, skin side down, for a minute, then flip over and cook the other side for another minute. Squeeze half a lemon over the fish. Place the fish on a warm dish and sprinkle with the almond stuffing.

4. To serve, toss the rocket with the piquillo peppers and fennel. Serve with the sardines and a wedge of lemon.

SOUTHERN INDIAN
SPICED FISH

This is based on a recipe in *Spice*, by Christine Manfield. Jane used to make this when she lived in Samoa. It's so easy.

PREP TIME: 15 MINS · COOK TIME: 30 MINS

1 teaspoon **ground turmeric**

1 teaspoon **cayenne pepper**

½ teaspoon **ground white pepper**

½ teaspoon **salt**

700g **hake fillets**, skinned (or **other white fish**)

3 tablespoons **rapeseed oil**

1 × 2cm piece of **ginger**, finely grated

3 **cardamom pods**, crushed

3 **onions**, sliced

3 cloves of **garlic**, crushed

4 **green chillies**, sliced

1 teaspoon **ground coriander**

150ml **fish stock**

400ml **coconut milk**

2 tablespoons **mustard seeds**

2 sprigs of **curry leaves**

salt and **freshly ground black pepper**

TO SERVE

juice of 1 **lime**

fresh coriander leaves

1. Mix together the turmeric, cayenne, pepper and salt. Cut the fish into large 4cm pieces and rub with the spice mix. Heat 2 tablespoons of oil in a large non-stick frying pan and cook the fish pieces for a minute on each side. Remove from the pan and set aside.

2. Put the ginger, cardamom, onions, garlic and chillies into the pan and cook over a low heat for 15 minutes, without browning. Add the ground coriander, fish stock and coconut milk. Bring up to a simmer and cook for 5 minutes. Return the fish to the pan and cook gently for 5 minutes, or until the fish is just cooked (this will depend on the thickness of the fillets).

3. Heat the remaining tablespoon of oil in another pan and add the mustard seeds and curry leaves. When the seeds start to pop, pour the contents of the pan into the coconut sauce and stir to combine.

4. Serve with a squeeze of lime juice and a sprinkling of coriander leaves.

CHERMOULAH MONKFISH

This North African spice blend is fantastic with fish, like Jane's friend (and restaurateur), Mitch Tonks. You'd traditionally use a chermoulah seasoning on lamb or chicken, but monkfish is so meaty that it can stand up to the bold flavour.

PREP TIME: 15 MINS · MARINATING TIME: OVERNIGHT
COOK TIME: 25 MINS

600g **monkfish tails**

1 tablespoons **olive oil**

2 **cardamom pods**, crushed

1 clove of **garlic**, crushed

1 × 2cm piece of **ginger**, grated

4 large **tomatoes**, skinned and chopped

100g **cooked Puy lentils**

100ml **fish stock**

2 tablespoons chopped **fresh coriander**

50g **watercress**

salt and **freshly ground black pepper**

FOR THE CHERMOULAH MARINADE

1 teaspoon **ground coriander**

1 teaspoon **ground cumin**

1 teaspoon **ground fennel seeds**

juice of ½ **lemon**

1 tablespoon **red wine vinegar**

1 clove of **garlic**, crushed

1 **red chilli**, finely chopped

1 teaspoon **coconut sugar**

1 teaspoon **smoked paprika**

1. Mix together all the marinade ingredients. Place the monkfish in the marinade and leave in the refrigerator for a few hours or overnight.

2. Heat a tablespoon of olive oil in a pan and add the cardamom, garlic and ginger. Cook for 2 minutes over a low heat, then add the chopped tomatoes. Turn the heat up and cook for 10 minutes, until you have a thick sauce. Stir in the lentils and fish stock and bring to a simmer. Cook for a few minutes, then season well and stir in the fresh coriander.

3. Heat a griddle plate until very hot. Remove the monkfish from its marinade and grill for about 5 minutes, turning to make sure all sides are browned.

4. When the tails are firm to touch, remove from the grill and leave to rest for a few minutes. The cooking time will depend on the size and thickness of the tails.

5. Slice the fish into 1–2cm pieces and arrange on top of the sauce with a little watercress to serve.

BRAISED CLAMS, MUSSELS, FENNEL, LEEKS & 'NDUJA

Chorizo can be used instead of 'nduja (a spicy, spreadable sausage), but it won't melt into the sauce like the soft Calabrian paste will.

PREP TIME: 10 MINS · COOK TIME: 15 MINS

2 **shallots**, sliced

2 **leeks**, sliced

2 heads of **fennel**, sliced

4 cloves of **garlic**, crushed

50g **'nduja**

3 tablespoons **olive oil**

1kg **mussels**, cleaned

1kg **clams**

100ml **white wine**

2 tablespoons chopped **fresh parsley**

1. Cook the shallots, leeks, fennel and garlic, with the 'nduja, in the olive oil for about 2 minutes. The 'nduja should dissolve on cooking.

2. Heat a large pan until very hot. Tip in the mussels and clams and pour in the white wine. Cover immediately and shake the pan. Cook for a few minutes, until all the shells start to open (discarding any shells that do not open). Immediately empty the shellfish into a colander over a bowl to collect the cooking liquor.

3. Pour the liquor into the fennel mix and bring to a simmer. Cook for 5 minutes, then stir in the mussels and clams. Serve sprinkled with plenty of chopped parsley.

BEAN & SAUERKRAUT SOUP

This soup is a bit unusual, but will soon become something you make all the time. It's long been known that sauerkraut is oh-so-good for you. It aids digestion, is full of good bacteria and has even been known to have cancer-fighting properties.

**PREP TIME: 20 MINS · SOAKING TIME: OVERNIGHT
COOK TIME: 1 HOUR**

200g **borlotti beans**, soaked overnight in lots of **cold water**

10 cloves of **garlic**, 6 peeled and left whole, 4 crushed

2 **bay leaves**

4 **cherry tomatoes**

500g **kohlrabi**, peeled and diced

2 tablespoons **olive oil**

2 **onions**, diced

2 teaspoons **caraway seeds**, crushed

1 tablespoon **paprika**

300g **sauerkraut**, rinsed

2 tablespoons chopped **fresh parsley**

salt and **freshly ground black pepper**

1. Drain the beans and place in a pan. Cover with about a litre of water and add the whole cloves of garlic, bay leaves and tomatoes. Bring to the boil, then simmer for about 40 minutes, making sure the beans are always covered with plenty of water.

2. Add the diced kohlrabi to the pan and simmer for another 20 minutes, or until the kohlrabi is cooked. Remove the bay leaves and mash the bean and kohlrabi mixture roughly with a potato masher. Take out a large cupful of the mix and blend and return it to the beans. Stir well and season.

3. While the beans are cooking, heat the oil in a pan and cook the onions for 10 minutes. Add the crushed cloves of garlic and caraway seeds and cook for a minute. Turn up the heat and stir in the paprika and sauerkraut. Stir-fry for a few minutes, then tip all the ingredients into the bean pan. Add a little water to the onion pan and scrape out into the soup pan.

4. Stir everything together, adding a little water or veg stock if the soup is too thick. Check the seasoning, and serve sprinkled with parsley.

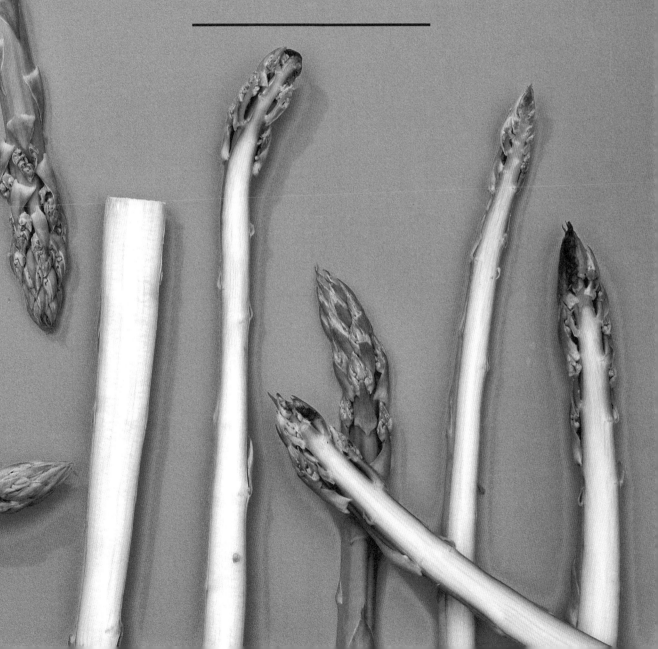

6

BITS ON THE SIDE

POTATO FOCACCIA

This recipe has quite a few steps, and takes patience, but the rewards couldn't be more worth it. A light, fluffy and magnificently hearty loaf based on a traditional Pugliese bread. We think it's best served sliced, toasted and with some of our top dips (see page 78).

PREP TIME: 20 MINS · RISE TIME: 40–60 MINS · COOK TIME: 45 MINS

300g **baking potatoes**

2 × 7g sachets of **fast-action dried yeast**

1 tablespoon **raw honey**

100ml **tepid water**

1 tablespoon **psyllium husks**

1 teaspoon **ground chia seeds**

1 teaspoon **ground flaxseeds**

400ml **cold water**

2 **egg whites**

4 tablespoons **olive oil**

10 **cherry tomatoes**, halved

1 tablespoon chopped **fresh rosemary**

sea salt

FOR THE FLOUR MIX

100g **sorghum flour**

100g **millet flour**

100g **tapioca flour**

100g **polenta**

100g **arrowroot**

2 teaspoons **baking powder**

1 teaspoon **vitamin C powder**

1 teaspoon **salt**

1. Boil the baking potatoes in their jackets until tender.

2. Place all the flour mix ingredients in a large bowl. Mix the yeast with the honey and the tepid water. Mix the psyllium husks and ground seeds with the cold water.

3. When the potatoes are cool enough to handle, remove the skins and push the potatoes through a potato ricer into the bowl containing the flour. Rub together.

4. Whisk the egg whites until just holding soft peaks. Add the yeast mix to the psyllium mix and stir. Pour into the flour mix along with the egg whites and mix together until well combined. You should have quite a wet, sticky dough. Mix in half of the olive oil and leave to rise for 20 minutes.

5. Transfer the dough to a baking tray lined with baking parchment and spread out, using your fingers, into a rough oblong 2cm deep.

6. Top with the cherry tomatoes, skin side up, and sprinkle with the rosemary and sea salt. Leave in a warm place, to double in size. This should take about 20–40 minutes depending on how warm it is.

7. Heat the oven to 220°C/425°F/gas mark 7.

8. Drizzle the focaccia with the remaining olive oil and bake for 20–25 minutes, or until well browned and cooked through. Transfer to a cooling tray and allow to cool completely before slicing.

The focaccia slices can be grilled in a griddle pan – they crisp up all lovely.

CORN BREAD

100ml **coconut oil**, melted, plus extra for greasing

150g **polenta**

150g **masa harina**

2 teaspoons **baking powder**

1 teaspoon **sweet paprika**

1 teaspoon **smoked paprika**

a large pinch of **salt**

2 **eggs**

50g **rice malt syrup**

200ml **coconut milk**

sweetcorn kernels from 1 cob (optional)

Insert corny joke here. This is another recipe from our mates Meleni and Rob, who advise us at LEON about our nutrition. You can also add whole corn kernels for a bit of extra texture.

PREP TIME: 15 MINS · COOK TIME: 30 MINS

1. Heat the oven to 200°C/400°F/gas mark 6.

2. Mix together the dry ingredients. Separately, whisk the eggs lightly together and add the rest of the oil, syrup and coconut milk. Beat to combine.

3. Pour the wet ingredients into the dry and stir to combine. Add the corn kernels if using. Do not over-mix. Pour the batter into a 20cm square cake tin, greased with coconut oil and lined with baking parchment, and bake in the oven for 25–30 minutes. Serve warm or at room temperature.

PITTA PAN

30g **ground psyllium husks**

600ml **water**

750g **gluten-free bread flour**

3 tablespoons **sesame seeds**

1 tablespoon **ground fennel seeds**

1 tablespoon **raw honey**

1 tablespoon **salt**

20g **instant yeast**

3 **eggs**

1 tablespoon **white wine vinegar**

90ml **olive oil**

It'd be a real pity if you couldn't have pitta any more just because of gluten. Don't be put off by the psyllium husks. It's much more natural than it sounds. Made from plant husks, it helps to bind the ingredients in gluten-free bread and it's great for digestion. We prefer it to xanthan gum, which sometimes doesn't agree with people's tummies.

PREP TIME: 20 MINS · RISE TIME: 20 MINS
COOK TIME: 45 MINS

1. Mix the ground psyllium with 300ml of water. Set aside to thicken.

2. Tip the flour and seeds into a mixing bowl. Add the honey and salt to one side of the bowl and the yeast to the other. Crack the eggs into the centre of the flour, then add the vinegar, olive oil and the psyllium mixture. Combine to form a soft dough. Gradually add the remaining water, you may not need it all, the dough should be soft and slightly sticky.

3. Place on a floured surface and knead for a few minutes to form a smooth dough. Put back into the bowl, cover and leave to rest for 1½ hours, until doubled in size.

4. Heat the oven to 220°C/425°F/gas mark 7 and place 3 heavy-duty baking trays in the oven to heat up.

5. Dust your work surface with flour. Divide the dough into 12 equal pieces and shape each one into a ball. Roll or press the pieces into oval shapes about 4mm thick.

6. Remove the baking trays from the oven and dust with a little flour. Lay 4 pittas on each tray and bake for 10–12 minutes, until puffed up and cooked through. The pittas should have a slight colour to them. Remove from the oven and wrap in a clean tea towel to keep them soft until ready to serve.

Try these pittas with the fava bean purée on page 68.

COURGETTE SALAD

5 **courgettes**

juice of ½ **lemon**

2 tablespoons chopped **fresh mint**

2 tablespoons **olive oil**

1 **red chilli**, chopped

1 tablespoon finely chopped **black olives**

salt and **freshly ground black pepper**

It doesn't get much fresher than this.
As Mary Nightingale used to say on *Wish You Were Here*.

PREP TIME: 10 MINS · STAND TIME: 20 MINS

1. Finely julienne or grate the courgettes. Place in a colander and add about ½ teaspoon of salt. Mix together and leave for at least 20 minutes.

2. Squeeze out any excess moisture from the courgettes, then mix with the rest of the ingredients before serving.

PARSNIP QUINOA WITH HAZELNUTS, MINT & APRICOTS

250g **parsnips**, peeled and finely chopped

4 **dried apricots**, finely chopped

200g **quinoa**

1 tablespoon **olive oil**

2 tablespoons **hazelnuts**, crushed

2 tablespoons chopped **fresh mint**

1 tablespoon **lemon juice**

salt and **freshly ground black pepper**

Up your quinoa game with this parsnip-pimped version.

PREP TIME: 10 MINS · COOK TIME: 25 MINS

1. Place the parsnips and apricots in a pan. Cover with water and simmer for about 10 minutes, or until the parsnips are tender. Drain, reserving the cooking liquid in a measuring jug. Make up to 300ml with water.

2. Rinse the quinoa under running cold water and drain. Heat the oil in a pan and add the quinoa. Stir-fry for a minute and season. Add the 300ml of liquid and bring up to a simmer. Cover and cook for 15 minutes. Add the parsnips and apricots, then cover the pan and leave in a warm place for at least another 15 minutes.

3. Stir in the hazelnuts, mint and lemon juice. Season well before serving.

MARINATED AUBERGINE WEDGES

Live life on the wedge.

PREP TIME: 10 MINS · COOK TIME: 25 MINS

3 large **aubergines**, peeled with a
   paring knife

3 tablespoons **olive oil**

3 tablespoons **balsamic vinegar**

1 tablespoon **raw honey**

2 teaspoons **paprika**

3 cloves of **garlic**, finely chopped

3 **red chillies**, deseeded and
   chopped

1 tablespoon **mint**, chopped

75g **rocket**

50g **toasted pine nuts**

extra virgin olive oil, for drizzling

salt and **freshly ground black
   pepper**

1. Heat the oven to 180°C/350°F/gas mark 4.

2. Cut the aubergines in half to make two shorter cylinders. Cut each cylinder into 8–10 wedges.

3. Mix together the oil, vinegar, honey and paprika. Toss the aubergine wedges in this marinade and season well. Leave for about 30 minutes to marinate.

4. Tip the aubergines on to a baking tray lined with baking parchment and place in the oven for about 20 minutes, or until they are just tender. Sprinkle with the garlic and chillies. Return to the oven for another 5 minutes. Set to one side to cool down.

5. To serve, toss the aubergines with the mint and rocket and sprinkle with the pine nuts. Drizzle with extra virgin olive oil t o serve.

PANISSE

750ml **water**

½ teaspoon **ground fennel seeds**

1 teaspoon finely chopped **fresh rosemary**

½ teaspoon crushed **garlic**

a pinch of **chilli flakes**

2 teaspoons **olive oil**

½ teaspoon **salt**

200g **gram flour**, sieved

rapeseed oil, for frying

These are a French chickpea version of polenta chips. Serve with plenty of sea salt and freshly ground black pepper.

PREP TIME: 5 MINS · COOK TIME: 20 MINS

1. Pour the water into a pan and add the fennel seeds, rosemary, garlic, chilli flakes, olive oil and salt. Heat to a simmer and gradually tip in the sieved gram flour to avoid getting lumps. Whisk together, then stir constantly with a wooden spoon for about 10 minutes over a low heat.

2. The mixture should be smooth – if it isn't, use a sieve and push the mixture through. Pour it out on to a greased tray. Smooth with a palette knife until ½–1cm deep and allow to cool. Cut into short strips about 1–2 × 4cm.

3. Heat about 2cm of oil in a pan and fry the panisse fingers for a few minutes, until lightly browned and crisp all over. Drain on kitchen paper before serving.

SOCCA

200g **gram flour**, sieved

1 teaspoon **salt**

a pinch of **ground cumin**

1 teaspoon finely chopped **fresh rosemary**

200–250ml **water**

2 tablespoons **olive oil**, plus extra for cooking

This thin chickpea pancake is great to serve, cut into rough pieces, with drinks. An anchovy mayonnaise or tapenade alongside some braised greens would make a great accompaniment. We have cooked our socca in the oven, but it can be made directly on the hob or under a grill. The secret is to cook it as thin as possible on a hot surface so the results are very crisp.

PREP TIME: 10 MINS · STAND TIME: 2 HOURS
COOK TIME: 25 MINS

1. Heat the oven to 220°C/425°F/gas mark 7.

2. Place the flour in a large bowl with the salt, cumin and rosemary. Add the water, whisking until you have a smooth batter the consistency of single cream. Whisk in the olive oil. Leave for at least 2 hours – it can be made up to this point the night before.

3. Place a cast-iron frying pan in a hot oven for about 10 minutes. Carefully remove from the oven and drizzle with a tablespoon of olive oil. Whisk the batter and pour in enough to cover the pan in a thin layer. Put back into the oven for about 10 minutes, or until the edges and top are browning.

4. Slide out of the pan on to a board and cut into pieces to serve. Repeat with the rest of the batter and break into pieces to serve.

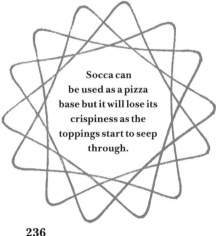

Socca can be used as a pizza base but it will lose its crispiness as the toppings start to seep through.

CARROT TOP PESTO & CARROTS

600g **carrots**, with fresh-looking tops

50ml **olive oil**, plus 1 tablespoon

1 teaspoon **raw honey**

1 small bunch of **fresh basil**

2 tablespoons **pine nuts**, toasted

1 clove of **garlic**, crushed

1 tablespoon **lemon** juice

salt and **freshly ground black pepper**

Jane has become slightly obsessed with 'vegetable offal' – the bits that we throw away but are truly marvellous. You could also try making crisps from vegetable peel, sautéeing cauliflower leaves or beet tops.

PREP TIME: 10 MINS · COOK TIME: 40 MINS

1. Heat the oven to 160°C/325°F/gas mark 3.

2. Cut the tops off the carrots, rinse and chop roughly.

3. Cut the carrots in half lengthways and toss with salt and pepper and 1 tablespoon of the olive oil. Place on a baking tray and drizzle with a little honey. Place in the oven for about 40 minutes, or until the carrots are tender.

4. Place the carrot tops in a food processor with the basil, pine nuts and garlic. Blitz to a rough paste and transfer to a bowl. Add the lemon juice and the 50ml of olive oil. Season the pesto to taste.

5. Arrange the carrots on a serving dish and drizzle with the pesto.

SQUASH & SAGE

400g **butternut squash**

3 tablespoons **olive oil**

2 cloves of **garlic**, thinly sliced

20 **fresh sage leaves**

2 tablespoons toasted **pine nuts**

a drizzle of **pumpkin seed oil**
   (optional)

salt and **freshly ground black
   pepper**

Fragrant sage and sweet squash – you'd be hard-pressed to find something so wholly autumnal as this.

PREP TIME: 10 MINS · COOK TIME: 10 MINS

1. Using a speed peeler or mandolin, shave thin strips from the squash into a bowl. No need to peel it first.

2. Heat the oil in a large pan and cook the garlic and sage for 2 minutes without browning the garlic. Remove with a slotted spoon.

3. Tip the squash into the pan and turn up the heat. Cook for 3 minutes, stirring well. Cover, then turn the heat down low for 3 minutes, or until the squash is just cooked. Season well.

4. Stir in the garlic, sage and pine nuts and transfer to a serving dish. Drizzle with a little pumpkin seed oil, if you have it, to serve.

PITTA DI PATATE

This onion and potato bread recipe was taught to Jane by a charming lady, Gianna Greco, who has a cookery school in Lecce, Puglia. The original had some cheese and breadcrumbs, but we tried it with toasted almonds and it was a roaring success. It is generally served slightly warm as part of an antipasti spread.

PREP TIME: 15 MINS · COOK TIME: 1 HOUR 40 MINS

6 **onions**, halved and thinly sliced

2 tablespoons **olive oil**, plus extra for greasing and drizzling

3 tablespoons **tomato passata** (or **chopped** and **peeled tomatoes**)

3 tablespoons **salted capers**, soaked in **cold water**

1 tablespoon shredded **fresh basil**

1kg **potatoes** (bakers, or a variety good for mash)

2 **eggs**, beaten

70g **ground almonds**

2 tablespoons chopped **fresh parsley**

2 tablespoons chopped **fresh chives**

salt and **freshly ground black pepper**

1. Heat the oven to 200°C/400°F/gas mark 6.

2. Place the onions in a large shallow pan with the olive oil and cook over a medium heat for about 10 minutes, without colouring. Add about 200ml of water, bring to a simmer and continue to cook gently for about 45 minutes. The longer you can cook the onions, the better flavour in the resulting dish.

3. Add the tomato passata and drained capers and cook for another 15 minutes. Stir in the basil.

4. While the onions are cooking, boil the potatoes in their skins until tender, then drain. When the potatoes are cool enough to handle, peel off the skins.

5. Pass the potatoes through a potato ricer into a large bowl and beat in the eggs. Lightly toast half the ground almonds and add to the bowl with the herbs. Season the potato mix very well.

6. Press half the potato mix into the bottom of a greased 22cm-square ovenproof dish to form a smooth layer. Top with the slow-cooked onions and any juices they may have. Add a final layer of potato and smooth down with a palette knife. Sprinkle with the rest of the almonds and drizzle with lots of olive oil.

7. Bake in the oven for about 30 minutes, or until the top is golden brown. Cut into squares to serve.

FERMENTED BEETROOT & FENNEL

1 litre **water**

20g **sea salt**

3–4 **beetroot**

1 head of **fennel**

½ teaspoon **fennel seeds**

This comes from our friend Jonny Guest, who was responsible for the sauerkraut recipe in *Fast Vegetarian*. Remember to loosen the lid every day for the first week of fermentation, to remove any gas. This will save you from an explosion.

PREP TIME: 10 MINS · FERMENTING TIME: 2 WEEKS

1. Mix the water with the salt until completely dissolved.

2. Wash and scrub the beetroot, then top and tail and finely slice. Trim the fennel and finely slice.

3. In a clean 1 litre jar, alternately layer the beetroot and the fennel with a few fennel seeds. Press down firmly. Cover completely with the brine and secure the lid. The vegetables must stay submerged in the brine for the fermentation to be successful.

4. Leave in a warm place for 2 weeks (loosening the lid every day for the first week), or until the vegetables are crunchy but have lost their 'rawness' and have a nice sour taste.

PATRA

These stuffed greens remind us of a Swiss roll. Serve with chutneys and dal, and you'll be greening from ear to ear. You can steam the rolls, leave them to cool, and keep in the refrigerator for hours until you're ready to fry.

PREP TIME: 40 MINS · COOK TIME: 40 MINS

1 bunch of **spring greens**

2 tablespoons **rice bran oil**

1 tablespoon **mustard seeds**

1 tablespoon **sesame seeds**

2 **onions**, thinly sliced

a pinch of **asafoetida**

FOR THE PASTE

150g **gram flour**

2 teaspoons **ground coriander**

1 teaspoon **ground cumin**

1 tablespoon **sesame seeds**

ground chilli powder, to taste

2cm of **ginger**, finely grated

2 **green chillies**, finely chopped

1 teaspoon **salt**

2 teaspoons **tamarind paste**

2 teaspoons **palm sugar**

2 tablespoons **rice bran oil**

100ml **water**

1. Separate the leaves of the spring greens and use a sharp knife to remove the thick part of the central rib.

2. Blend together all the paste ingredients in a food processor until you have a spreadable paste, adding more water if required.

3. Take 2 of the largest leaves and spread them out on a clean cloth or surface. Spread a thin layer of the paste on to each leaf. Top with another leaf. Repeat the process until all the paste has been used. Roll up each pile into a long thin tube. Place in a steamer (you may have to cut the rolls in half to fit them in) and steam for 25 minutes, or until they are firm to touch.

4. When cool, slice into rounds about 1–2cm thick. Heat the oil in a large frying pan. Add the mustard and sesame seeds. When the seeds start to pop, add the onions and asafoetida. Cook for 5 minutes, then remove from the pan with a slotted spoon and set aside. Start browning the patra slices for a few minutes each side, adding more oil if needed. When all the patra slices are browned, toss together with the onions and seeds and serve.

TRUFFLE PARSNIP FRIES

P
NF
V
Ve
SF

Keep your eyes on the fries. Seriously. If you're not careful, everyone'll pinch 'em.

PREP TIME: 5 MINS · COOK TIME: 30 MINS

6 large **parsnips**, peeled

2 tablespoons **olive oil**

salt and **freshly ground black pepper**

TO FINISH

a drizzle of **truffle oil**

a sprinkle of **truffle salt**

2 tablespoons chopped **fresh chives**

1. Heat the oven to 190°C/375°F/gas mark 5.

2. Cut the parsnips into chips or wedges about 1cm thick. Toss with the olive oil and season. Place on a baking tray lined with baking parchment and cook in the oven for about 20 minutes. Check the parsnips, give the tray a shake, and return to the oven for an extra 10 minutes if they are not quite cooked.

3. Scoop the parsnips off the tray and on to a serving dish. Drizzle with truffle oil and sprinkle with truffle salt and chives to serve.

We served these with a dollop of (non-vegan) truffle honey, which goes so well with the sweet parsnips.

SWEET POTATO GRATIN

This gratin is great in all scenarios.

PREP TIME: 10 MINS · COOK TIME: 45 MINS

1kg **sweet potatoes**, peeled

250ml **unsweetened almond milk**

3 cloves of **garlic**, crushed

2 **red chillies**, chopped

2 tablespoons finely chopped **fresh rosemary**

1 teaspoon **arrowroot**

salt and **freshly ground black pepper**

1. Heat the oven to 160°C/325°F/gas mark 3.

2. Thinly slice the sweet potatoes, season, and layer in a 25cm ovenproof gratin dish or similar.

3. Heat the almond milk with the garlic, chillies and rosemary and whisk together. Simmer for a few minutes to reduce a little, then mix the arrowroot with a tablespoon of water and whisk into the liquid to make a sauce.

4. Season the sauce and pour over the sweet potatoes. Cover the dish with foil and bake in the oven for about 40 minutes, or until the sweet potatoes are tender. Leave to cool slightly before serving.

BEETROOT GRATIN

This vivid purple gratin is incredible with smoked fish or roast beef. A step in the right direction for eating the rainbow.

PREP TIME: 10 MINS · COOK TIME: 55 MINS

1kg **beetroot**

1 tablespoon **olive oil**

2 **shallots**, finely chopped

1 clove of **garlic**, crushed

1 tablespoon chopped **fresh savory**

1 tablespoon **crushed pink peppercorns**

2 tablespoons grated **horseradish**

100ml **vegetable stock**

salt

1. Heat the oven to 160°C/325°F/gas mark 3.

2. Peel and finely slice the beetroot.

3. Heat the olive oil in a pan and add the shallots. Cook over a low heat for 10 minutes. Stir in the garlic, savory, peppercorns and horseradish. Cook for a minute, then add the stock. Bring to the boil, then simmer for 5 minutes.

4. Add the beetroot and season with salt. Mix well and layer up in a 25cm ovenproof gratin dish or similar. Cover tightly with foil, place in the oven, and cook for about 40 minutes, or until the beetroot is tender. Leave to cool slightly before serving.

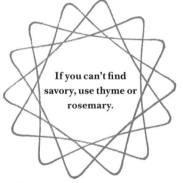

If you can't find savory, use thyme or rosemary.

BITS ON THE SIDE

CORN TORTILLAS & DIPS

:·10·:

Masa harina is a traditional Mexican flour made from ground corn kernels. Perfect for taco night, or try baking them with a little oil to make your own tortilla chips.

PREP TIME: 15 MINS · REST TIME: 30 MINUTES · COOK TIME: 30 MINS

150g **masa harina**

1 tablespoon **olive oil**

175ml **hot water**

salt

1. Place the masa harina in a bowl with a pinch of salt. Stir in the oil, then slowly add the hot water until you have a smooth dough. Knead for a while to bring together. Add more masa if it's too sticky, more water if too dry.

2. Leave to rest for about 30 minutes. Divide into 10 balls and roll out into small tortillas. This can be done using a tortilla press or with a rolling pin. If using a tortilla press, place the flattened ball between 2 sheets of baking parchment and place in the press to flatten.

3. Cook the tortillas as you press them. Heat a non-stick frying pan or cast-iron griddle until very hot, and cook them for about 2 minutes either side, until lightly browned and toasted.

4. Serve warm, with tomatillo salsa and avocado dip (see below).

TOMATILLO SALSA

PREP TIME: 10 MINS

1 clove of **garlic**, crushed

4 **jalapeño chillies**, chopped

400g **tomatillos**, chopped (You can use skinned ripe tomatoes if tomatillos aren't available.)

6 **spring onions**, chopped

juice of ½ **lime**

1 teaspoon **maple syrup**

2 tablespoons chopped **fresh coriander**

salt

1. Mix all the ingredients together in a bowl and season with salt. This should keep in a sealed container in the refrigerator for up to 3 days.

AVOCADO DIP

PREP TIME: 5 MINS

2 ripe **avocados**

1 clove of **garlic**

1 teaspoon **chipotle paste**

50ml **olive oil**

juice of ½ **lime**

salt and **freshly ground black pepper**

1. Blend all the ingredients together until smooth, and season. This should keep in a sealed container in the refrigerator for a day.

ETHIOPIAN FLAT BREAD

This injera flat bread is normally made by a longer fermentation method, but we've sped it up for convenience and the results are good. This is normally served with a dal-like stew. A kachumber salad (see page 254) would complete the meal.

PREP TIME: 15 MINS · REST TIME: 1 HOUR · COOK TIME: 30 MINS

1 tablespoon **dried yeast**

150ml **warm water**

100g **teff flour**

½ teaspoon **baking powder**

1 teaspoon **cider vinegar**

100ml **cold water**

rice bran oil, for greasing

salt

1. Blend the yeast with the warm water. Mix with the flour and set aside for an hour. Whisk in the baking powder, vinegar, salt and cold water so you have a thin batter.

2. Heat a non-stick frying pan or griddle plate. Grease the pan using a cloth or a piece of kitchen paper dipped in oil. Ladle a little of the batter on to the pan and spread out either by using the ladle or tilting the pan.

3. Cover the pan for a minute to steam, uncover, then cook for another 3 minutes. Repeat with the rest of the batter and serve.

RED LENTIL STEW

PREP TIME: 5 MINS · COOK TIME: 45 MINS

2 **onions**, chopped

2 tablespoons **rice bran oil**

5 tablespoons **berbere spice mix**

1 tablespoon grated **ginger**

2 cloves of **garlic**, crushed

250g **red lentils**, rinsed well

75ml **water**

1 teaspoon **salt**

1. In a large pan cook the onions in the oil for 10 minutes. Add the spice mix, ginger and garlic and cook for another 3 minutes.

2. Add the lentils and stir well to combine. Pour in the water and bring to a simmer, then cook for 30 minutes, until the lentils have gone slightly mushy. Season with the salt and serve with the Ethiopian flatbread.

SANDWICH BREAD

After many, many attempts – this is the one. Jane's been through a lot. She tried one, and thought she had nailed it. It rose beautifully, but when she cut into it there was nothing inside. Just a hole. She stuck with it, though, and this bread is the perfect proof of persistence. We love it toasted, or as a BLT.

PREP TIME: 10 MINS · RISE TIME: 45–55 MINUTES · COOK TIME: 40 MINS

600ml **lukewarm water**

3 teaspoons **dried yeast**

2 teaspoons **raw honey**

100g **millet flour**

100g **sorghum flour**

100g **chestnut flour**

80g **quinoa flour**

1 teaspoon **salt**

20g **psyllium husks**

20g **ground chia seeds**

3 tablespoons **olive oil**, plus extra for greasing

1. Mix the water with the yeast and honey. Set aside for about 15 minutes.

2. In a large bowl, mix together all the dry ingredients.

3. Add the olive oil to the yeast solution. Pour on to the dry ingredients and bring together to make a soft dough. Turn out on to a clean surface and knead lightly for a few minutes, adding a little extra flour if required. Place in a greased 450g-loaf tin lined with baking parchment and leave for 30–40 minutes until the loaf has doubled in size.

4. Heat the oven to 220°C/425°F/gas mark 7.

5. Cook the loaf in the oven for about 40 minutes. If it browns too much on top, cover with foil.

6. Remove from the oven and allow to cool in the tin.

You can use regular gluten-free flour, but we made a mix here that's more nutritious and tasty.

SPICED CHICKPEAS

These are a great little bar (or sofa) snack.

PREP TIME: 5 MINS · COOK TIME: 30 MINS

2 × 400g tins of **chickpeas**, drained

2 tablespoons **olive oil**

½ teaspoon **ground cumin**

1 teaspoon **freshly ground black pepper**

chilli powder, to taste

½ teaspoon **smoked paprika**

salt

1. Heat the oven to 200°C/400°F/gas mark 6.

2. Rinse the chickpeas well under cold running water, then drain and dry with clean tea towels or kitchen roll.

3. Put the chickpeas into a bowl and toss with the olive oil. Mix together the rest of the ingredients and toss through the chickpeas.

4. Place on a baking tray lined with baking parchment and roast in the preheated oven for about 30 minutes, giving the tray a shake after 15 minutes. When the chickpeas are crisp, turn off the oven but leave them inside the oven to cool down before serving.

KACHUMBER SALAD

This is such a great go-to side salad. It lends itself to Indian, Middle Eastern and European dishes. It's a total all-rounder.

PREP TIME: 10 MINS

250g **tomatoes**, chopped

1 **red onion**, finely chopped

¼ **cucumber**, peeled and chopped

1 teaspoon **cumin seeds**, toasted and ground

1 tablespoon chopped **fresh coriander**

1 tablespoon chopped **fresh mint**

1 **green chilli**, chopped

1 tablespoon **balsamic vinegar**

½ teaspoon **salt**

a pinch of **cayenne pepper**

1. Mix all the ingredients together in a bowl.

Mix the spiced chickpeas with some kachumber salad, crushed peanuts and tortilla chips for a bhel puri type salad.

You can change the spicing on these chickpeas: try them with Indian spices like garam masala, or Mexican spices like chilli and coriander.

7

TREAT YOURSELF

TROPICAL TRIFLE

A slightly boozy trip down Memory Lane. We've added a splash of Malibu to the custard because it's John's tropical tipple of choice. He is largely from the 80s. This dessert wibbles while you wobble.

PREP TIME: 15 MINS · CHILL TIME: A FEW HOURS · COOK TIME: 15 MINS

½ quantity **basic sponge recipe**
   (see page 262)

50ml **spiced rum**

1 **mango**, peeled and diced

¼ **pineapple**, peeled and diced

300ml **coconut cream**

toasted **coconut pieces**

FOR THE JELLY

2 tablespoons **agar agar**

100ml **boiling water**

4 tablespoons **brown rice syrup**

400ml **orange** or **blood orange**
   juice

FOR THE COCONUT CUSTARD

6 **egg yolks**

1 tablespoon **palm sugar**

2 teaspoons **cornflour**

300ml **coconut milk**

a splash of **Malibu**

FOR THE PASSION FRUIT CURD

7 **passion fruits**

50g **coconut oil**

50g **coconut sugar**

1 **egg**

2 **egg yolks**

1. Cut the sponge into chunks and place in the bottom of a large glass trifle dish. Drizzle with the rum and top with the fruit. Place the coconut cream in a bowl in the refrigerator.

2. Heat the agar agar flakes with the water and syrup. Simmer for 2 minutes, until the flakes have dissolved. Stir in the orange juice. Allow to cool a little, then pour over the fruit. Transfer the dish to the refrigerator to allow the jelly to set (this may take a few hours).

3. Whisk the egg yolks with the sugar and cornflour until smooth. Heat the coconut milk until it is just about to boil. Pour on to the egg yolks and whisk to combine. Return the mixture to the pan and cook over a very low heat until the custard is of coating consistency, about 5 minutes. Add Malibu to taste, and set aside to cool.

4. Blitz the pulp from 5 of the passion fruits, then sieve to remove the seeds. Combine the juice with the coconut oil, sugar, egg and yolks in a pan. Whisk together and cook gently over a low heat until the mixture thickens, about 5 minutes. Stir in the pulp and seeds from the 2 remaining passion fruit. Allow to cool.

5. Spread the passion fruit curd over the cold orange jelly and top with the custard. Whisk up the chilled coconut cream and spoon on top of the trifle. Sprinkle with toasted coconut to serve.

Agar agar is made from seaweed, and we love it. If you only have gelatine to hand, you can substitute equal amounts, but remember it won't be vegetarian.

STICKY TOFFEE PUDDING

We've probably never encountered a soul who wouldn't put their hand up for a bit of sticky toffee pudding. It's all in the name. Sticky. Toffee. Pudding. And now 'free-from friends' will put their hand up too. This recipe is adapted from the Macrobiotic School in Totnes, which is near Jane's house.

PREP TIME: 15 MINS · COOK TIME: 1 HOUR

FOR THE TOFFEE SAUCE

125ml **maple syrup**

125ml **rice malt syrup**

a small pinch of **sea salt**

150ml **non-dairy cream** (e.g. **soya**)

FOR THE PUDDING

12 **dates**, pitted and finely chopped

8 **dried apricots**, finely chopped

1 teaspoon **bicarbonate of soda**

50ml **coconut oil**

125ml **almond milk**

½ tsp **vanilla extract**

50ml **maple syrup**

2 tablespoons **date syrup**

200g **gluten-free self-raising flour**

1 teaspoon **baking powder**

200ml **almond milk**

1 teaspoon **vanilla extract**

2 **egg yolks**

2 teaspoons **cornflour**

2 tablespoons **coconut sugar**

1. Boil the maple syrup, rice malt syrup and salt together until you get a thick syrup.

2. Add the cream and reduce by one third to a half, or until it tastes like toffee sauce.

3. Pour into an 1½-litre ovenproof pudding bowl and allow to cool.

4. Put the dates, apricots and bicarbonate of soda into a bowl and pour over just enough boiling water to cover. Leave for 30 minutes to soften.

5. Heat the oven to 180°C/350°F/gas mark 4.

6. Mix all the wet ingredients together. Sieve the self-raising flour and baking powder into a mixing bowl, then pour over the wet ingredients and stir until smooth. Add the soaked fruit (don't drain it).

7. Pour the mixture evenly on top of the sauce in the ovenproof dish and bake in the oven for about 30 minutes, or until an inserted cocktail stick comes out clean. Serve with almond milk custard (see below).

ALMOND MILK CUSTARD

PREP TIME: 10 MINS · COOK TIME: 5 MINS

1. Bring the almond milk and vanilla extract to the boil.

2. In a bowl, mix the yolks, cornflour and sugar. Add the hot milk and whisk until it thickens. If it doesn't thicken enough, put it back into the pan and place on the hob over a low heat for a few minutes. Sieve before serving.

VICTORIA SPONGE

Put a spring in your step with this sponge.

PREP TIME: 10 MINS · COOK TIME: 30 MINS · CHILL TIME: 10 MINS

FOR THE SPONGE CAKES

400g **soya margarine**

200g **coconut sugar**

100g **brown rice syrup**

2 teaspoons **vanilla extract**

8 **eggs**

400g **gluten-free self-raising flour**

2 teaspoons **baking powder**

4 teaspoons **modified tapioca
   starch** (or **baking fix**), optional

TO SERVE

1 serving **vanilla cashew cream**
   (see page 270)

150g **raspberries**, plus extra to
   decorate

a handful of assorted **edible
   flowers**

1 tablespoon **dessicated coconut**

1. Heat the oven to 160°C/325°F/gas mark 3.

2. Cream together the soya margarine and the coconut sugar. Whisk in the rice syrup and the vanilla extract. Add the eggs one by one, whisking well after each addition.

3. Sift together the rest of the sponge cake ingredients and fold into the cake mix. Pour into a couple of 24cm cake tins lined with baking parchment and bake in the oven for about 30 minutes, or until a skewer comes out of the cakes clean. Transfer to a cooling rack and allow to cool for 10 minutes, then remove from the tin to finish cooling.

4. Once cooled, spread the vanilla cashew cream onto one cake and top with the raspberries. Add the second sponge on top and decorate with extra raspberries, edible flowers and a dusting of dessicated coconut to serve.

RAW CASHEW 'CHEESE' CAKE

Have your raw no-bake cake and eat it too. We recommend you use a 20cm loose-bottomed cake tin. This is a recipe from Jane's friend Carrie Allcot, who she used to work with – she's not sure where the recipe came from, but we're so glad it's here. A real show stopper.

PREP TIME: 30 MINS · SOAK TIME: OVERNIGHT · FREEZE TIME: A FEW HOURS

FOR THE BASE

200g **soft dates**

100g **ground almonds**

2 teaspoons **date syrup**

25g **sugar-free dark chocolate**, grated

FOR THE FILLING

250g **raw cashew nuts**, soaked overnight in lots of **cold water**

juice of 4 **lemons**

1 teaspoon **vanilla extract** (or seeds from a **vanilla pod**)

100g **coconut oil**, melted

100g **raw honey**

100g **raspberries**, plus extra to decorate

100g **beetroot**, peeled and cooked

1. To make the base, finely chop the dates and mix with the almonds, date syrup and chocolate. Line a 24cm cake tin with baking parchment and press the base mix into the bottom of the tin – use your hands, it makes it much easier. Keep in the refrigerator until the filling is ready.

2. Drain the nuts very well and place in a food processor with the lemon juice, vanilla, melted coconut oil and honey. Blend until very smooth. A powerful blender will achieve smoother results.

3. Divide the mix into 3. Blend one third with the raspberries, one with the beetroot and leave the other plain.

4. Layer up the 3 coloured purées on top of the cake base – or you could swirl them together. Place in the freezer to set. Serve decorated with the extra berries.

Try mixing different fruit or vegetables with the cashew cream to get a different spectrum of colour – try blackberries and blueberries or avocados and kiwi.

MANGO-GO

Another one from Carrie Allcot. Man, go make this delightfully dense pudding cake. Make sure you check the packets of your dried fruit though, there can often be sneakily added sugar.

PREP TIME: 20 MINS · STAND TIME: OVER NIGHT · COOK TIME: 50 MINS

125g **dried mango**

125g **dried apricots**

300ml **boiling water**

1½ teaspoons **bicarbonate of soda**

200g **rice flour**

125g **macadamia nuts**, ground

1 teaspoon **ground cinnamon**

1 teaspoon **ground ginger**

1 teaspoon **baking powder**

100g **ripe bananas** (about
    1 banana)

150ml **melted coconut oil**

a few drops of **vanilla extract**

a few tablespoons of **almond milk**

2 **mangoes**, cut into cubes, to serve

1. Heat the oven to 180°C/350°F/gas mark 4.

2. Place the dried fruit in a bowl. Pour over the water, add 1 teaspoon of bicarbonate of soda and give the mix a stir. Leave overnight to soften.

3. Blend the fruit with the soaking water to make a thick purée. Empty the purée into a large bowl and sift in all the remaining dry ingredients.

4. Blitz the bananas in a food processor until smooth. Slowly add the melted coconut oil until you have an emulsion. Tip into the bowl, along with the other ½ teaspoon of bicarbonate of soda and the vanilla extract. Fold all the ingredients together, adding almond milk until you have a dropping consistency.

5. Pour the cake mix into a 450g loaf tin or a 20cm cake tin lined with baking parchment and bake in the oven for 30 minutes, then reduce the oven temperature to 160°C/325°F/gas mark 3 and cook for a further 20 minutes.

6. Allow to cool before turning out. Serve with fresh mango.

This would be totally tropical served with grilled pineapple and pineapple, banana and coconut ice cream (see page 292).

MOIST CHOCOLATE & ALMOND CAKES

These recipes are from Jane's lovely friend Emily Vevers, who runs Queen Bee Cakes in Devon. Moist is on our funny word list.

PREP TIME: 20 MINS · COOK TIME: 15 MINS

105g **coconut oil**, melted, plus extra for greasing

25g **ground almonds**

4 **eggs**

165g **coconut sugar**

175g **sugar-free dark chocolate**

25g **rice flour**

½ teaspoon **vanilla extract**

50ml **water**

dried cherries, finely chopped to decorate (optional)

FOR THE ICING

90g **sugar-free dark chocolate**

25g **coconut oil**

20g **raw honey**

1. Heat the oven to 160°C/325°F/gas mark 3.

2. Grease 2 trays of 12 mini cake moulds or fairy cake tins (depending on what you have available) and line with paper cases.

3. Chop the chocolate finely (using a food processor or by hand) and place in a large bowl. Add the rice flour and ground almonds and set aside.

4. Whisk the eggs and sugar together until pale and fluffy, then set aside.

5. Place the coconut oil, vanilla and measured water in a pan and bring to the boil. Pour this over the chocolate mix.

6. Whisk together until all the chocolate melts, then let cool. Fold in the egg mixture. Bake in the oven for 10–15 minutes, until well risen and no longer soft to touch in the middle.

7. Leave to cool slightly in the tin, and when cool enough to handle remove the tin and place the cakes on a cooling rack. Leave to cool completely before icing.

8. For the icing, gently melt the chocolate, coconut oil and honey in a bain-marie. Leave to cool and solidify slightly, then coat each cake with the icing. Decorate and leave to set before serving.

These cakes can be decorated with fresh summer berries, chopped pistachio nuts, chocolate curls, candied orange peel and lots more – it's your chance for creative caking.

GRILLED PEACHES WITH CASHEW CREAM

Just peachy.

**PREP TIME: 10 MINS · SOAK TIME: OVERNIGHT
COOK TIME: 6 MINS**

150g **cashew nuts**, soaked overnight in plenty of **cold water**, then drained

1 teaspoon **vanilla extract**

2 tablespoons **raw honey**

150g **raspberries**

juice of 1 **orange**

2 teaspoons **coconut sugar**

4 **peaches**, halved

a drizzle of **amaretto** or **brandy**

50g **almonds**, toasted

1. Blend the nuts in a food processor with about 125ml water until smooth. Add the vanilla and honey and continue to blend until you have the consistency of very thick cream. Place in the refrigerator.

2. Blitz the raspberries with the orange juice and sugar. Strain through a sieve or muslin to make a smooth sauce.

3. Heat a griddle pan until very hot. Place the peach halves, cut side down, on the griddle and cook for a few minutes, until the peach flesh is charred and caramelized. Remove to a serving dish.

4. To serve, top the peaches with spoonfuls of cashew cream. Drizzle with raspberry sauce and amaretto, and sprinkle with toasted almonds to serve.

GOLDEN MERINGUES

Erythritol sounds super processed, but it's not. (Terrible naming, guys.) Naturally occurring, it has 95 per cent fewer calories than sugar.

PREP TIME: 10 MINS · COOK TIME: 1 HOUR 20 MINS

2 **egg whites**

3 tablespoons **erythritol**, ground

few drops of **vanilla extract**

½ teaspoon **cream of tartar**

a pinch of **salt**

You need a dry oven to make meringues. Ideally you shouldn't have recently cooked anything in it.

1. Heat the oven to 120°C/250°F/gas mark ½.

2. Place all the ingredients in a cold metal or glass bowl. Using an electric mixer, whisk together for a few minutes, or until the mix is stiff and glossy.

3. Spoon small mounds on to a baking tray lined with baking parchment. Place in the oven and bake for about 20 minutes, then lower the temperature to 100°C/225°F/gas mark ¼ and leave in the oven for another hour or so, until the meringues are crisp. The length of time will depend on your oven.

4. Turn the heat off, but leave the meringues to cool in the oven before serving with peaches and cashew cream, if liked.

CHOCOLATE MAYO BROWNIES

coconut oil, for greasing

3 eggs

100g coconut sugar

100g mayonnaise

50g rice flour

25g ground almonds

1 teaspoon baking powder

50g chopped pecans

250g sugar-free dark chocolate, chopped into small pieces and melted

Before you think it, yes, these are great. You may not want to tell people what your secret ingredient is, but we think the rich moistness it adds is better than butter.

PREP TIME: 15 MINS · COOK TIME: 15 MINS

1. Heat the oven to 160°C/325°F/gas mark 3.

2. Grease a 22cm cake tin with coconut oil and line with baking parchment – this is to make sure the parchment sticks.

3. Whisk together the eggs and coconut sugar. Whisk in the mayonnaise. Fold in the dry ingredients, chopped nuts and melted chocolate.

4. Pour the cake batter into the tin and bake for about 15 minutes, until just cooked. Remove from the oven and allow to sit for 5 minutes, then turn out onto a cooling rack. Cut into wedges or squares to serve.

BEANIE (BABY) BROWNIES

250g sugar-free dark chocolate, chopped into small pieces and melted

400g tin cooked haricot beans, drained and rinsed

4 eggs

a few drops of vanilla extract

120g coconut sugar

1 teaspoon baking powder

These high-protein brownies, pumped up with haricot beans, deserve to be honoured. A recipe from our friend Meleni Aldridge.

PREP TIME: 15 MINS · COOK TIME: 40 MINS

1. Heat the oven to 170°C/350°F/gas mark 3.

2. Blitz the haricot beans in a food processor with the eggs and vanilla. Transfer to a bowl, add the sugar and baking powder, and stir well to combine. Stir in the melted chocolate.

3. Pour into a 22cm-square cake tin lined with baking parchment and bake in the oven for about 20 minutes. Leave to cool in the tin and, once completely cooled, cut into rectangles to serve.

SUMMER SCONES

These rhubarb and strawberry scones will be made today, scone tomorrow. A glorious pun from Polly Richards, a wonderful LEON intern.

PREP TIME: 15 MINS · COOK TIME: 15 MINS

100g **gluten-free plain flour**

100g **ground almonds**

1 tablespoon **modified tapioca starch** (or **baking fix**)

2 teaspoons **baking powder**

50g **coconut oil**

100g **coconut sugar**, plus extra for sprinkling

a pinch of **salt**

zest and juice of 1 **orange**

150g **rhubarb**, cut into 1cm pieces

100g **strawberries**, quartered

1 teaspoon **cornflour**

1 **egg**

2 tablespoons **maple syrup**

about 50ml **almond milk**, plus extra for glazing

1. Heat the oven to 200°C/400°F/gas mark 6.

2. Mix together the flour, ground almonds, starch and baking powder. Cut the solidified coconut oil into small pieces and rub into the dry ingredients until they resemble breadcrumbs. This can be done in a food processor

3. Grind the 100g of coconut sugar until it is fine and stir into the mixture with the salt and orange zest.

4. Toss the rhubarb and strawberries in the cornflour and stir into the scone mix.

5. Whisk the egg together with the orange juice and maple syrup until well combined. Pour into a measuring jug and add almond milk to the 160ml level. Whisk to combine before adding to the dry scone mix. Bring together with a palette knife to form a very soft dough. Empty on to a baking tray lined with baking parchment and press out into a circle about 1–2cm thick. Cut into eighths and brush with a little extra almond milk.

6. Sprinkle with the remaining coconut sugar and place in the hot oven for about 15 minutes.

7. Serve warm or at room temperature.

When plums are in season you could use them in place of the rhubarb and strawberries.

LEMON POLENTA CAKE
WITH BLUEBERRIES

The texture of this lemon polenta cake is hard to beat. Crumbly, fluffy and intense. You'll be wanting to make polenty.

PREP TIME: 15 MINS · COOK TIME: 30 MINS

100g **ground almonds**

100g **polenta**

2 tablespoons **cornflour**, plus 1 teaspoon

1 teaspoon **baking powder**

½ teaspoon **bicarbonate of soda**

1 teaspoon **modified tapioca starch** (or **baking fix**)

a pinch of **salt**

zest of 2 **lemons**

3 **eggs**

50ml **brown rice syrup**

3 tablespoons **raw honey**

1 teaspoon **vanilla extract**

50ml **olive oil**

120ml **almond milk**

150g **blueberries**

1. Heat the oven to 180°C/350°F/gas mark 4.

2. In a large bowl, mix together the dry ingredients, except for the 1 teaspoon of cornflour, and add the lemon zest.

3. Whisk the eggs with the rice syrup and honey until pale. Whisk in the vanilla, olive oil and milk. Whisk into the dry ingredients.

4. Pour the batter into a 22cm cake tin lined with baking parchment. Toss the blueberries in the remaining cornflour and sprinkle over the cake mix. Bake in the oven for 30 minutes.

5. Remove from the oven and allow to cool in the tin for 10 minutes, then turn out on to a cooling rack.

PISTACHIO CAKE
WITH POACHED APRICOTS

Stash a secret slice of this cake somewhere safe. It'll be gone before you've had a chance to tuck in.

PREP TIME: 10 MINS · COOK TIME: 50 MINS

3 **eggs**, beaten

zest of 2 **oranges**

150g **coconut sugar**

150ml **olive oil**

200g **ground pistachios**

50g **cornmeal**

1 teaspoon **baking powder**

a pinch of **ground cardamom**

1. Heat the oven to 180°C/350°F/gas mark 4.

2. Whisk the eggs with the orange zest and sugar. Add the olive oil and whisk together to combine.

3. Mix the pistachios with the cornmeal, baking powder and cardamom. Fold into the egg mixture and pour the batter into a 20cm round cake tin lined with baking parchment.

4. Bake for about 50 minutes, or until a skewer comes out clean. Allow to cool in the tin for 10 minutes, then turn out on to a cooling rack.

Cornmeal is like fine polenta – don't get it confused with cornflour.

POACHED APRICOTS

PREP TIME: 10 MINS · COOK TIME: 5 MINS

50ml **brown rice syrup**

100ml **sweet wine**

juice of 1 **orange**

400g **fresh apricots**, halved and stone removed

1. Bring the syrup, wine and orange juice to a simmer. Place the apricots in the syrup and cook for about 5 minutes.

2. Take the fruit out of the syrup with a slotted spoon and allow the syrup to simmer until it has reduced by half, about 5 minutes.

3. Pour the syrup over the fruit and serve.

TUSCAN CHESTNUT CAKE

Waste nut want nut, this is a naturally free-from recipe from Tuscany. Be transported to southern Italy. It helps if you have a few sunflowers lying around.

PREP TIME: 10 MINS · COOK TIME: 30 MINS

50g **golden raisins**

vin santo (optional)

250g **chestnut flour**

a pinch of **salt**

2 tablespoons **brown rice syrup**

2 tablespoons **olive oil**

20g **pine nuts**

20g **walnuts**

1 tablespoon roughly chopped
   fresh rosemary

1. Heat the oven to 180°C/350°F/gas mark 4.

2. Soak the raisins ahead of time – this can be done by covering them in hot water, or with vin santo or another sweet wine if available.

3. Sift the flour into a large bowl with the salt. Drain the liquid from the raisins into a measuring jug and make up the amount of liquid to 400ml. Add the liquid to the flour with the brown rice syrup, whisking to combine. Whisk in the olive oil and set aside for 30 minutes.

4. Whisk half the raisins into the cake mix. The batter should be of pouring consistency. Pour into a deep, 25cm baking tray lined with baking parchment to a depth of ½cm and sprinkle with the nuts, remaining raisins and rosemary. Bake in the oven for about 30 minutes. The top of the cake should have a cracked appearance.

5. Remove from the oven and allow to cool, then cut into slices or squares to serve.

JUMPING JACKS

These fruit and veg packed flapjacks will have you jumping for joy.

PREP TIME: 15 MINS · COOK TIME: 35 MINS

2 **carrots**

1 **parsnip**

1 **sweet potato**

1 **apple**

100g **cashew butter**

4 tablespoons **rice malt syrup**

50g **coconut sugar**

150g **gluten-free oats**

1 teaspoon **chia seeds**

1 teaspoon **flaxseeds**

1 tablespoon each of **pumpkin** and **sunflower seeds**

50g **desiccated coconut**

½ teaspoon **ground cinnamon**

1. Heat the oven to 180°C/350°F/gas mark 4.

2. Grate all the vegetables and the apple into a large bowl.

3. Melt the cashew butter with the syrup and coconut sugar in a pan over a low heat. Add the rest of the ingredients to the grated veg. Pour in the melted butter and stir to combine.

4. Spoon the mixture into a 20cm square cake tin or baking tray lined with baking parchment and press it down with the back of a spoon. It should be about 2cm deep.

5. Bake for about 30 minutes. Before the mix has cooled completely, cut into squares to serve.

CHESTNUT CHOC CHIP COOKIES

Oh, this old chestnut? They're best served warm and gooey.

PREP TIME: 10 MINS · COOK TIME: 15 MINS

2 **eggs**

100ml **coconut oil**, melted

50ml **rice malt syrup**

1 teaspoon **vanilla extract**

100g **chestnut flour**

50g **coconut flour**

1 teaspoon **bicarbonate of soda**

100g **sugar-free dark chocolate chips**

1. Heat the oven to 180°C/350°F/gas mark 4.

2. Whisk the eggs with the oil, syrup and vanilla in a large bowl.

3. Sieve the flours with the bicarbonate of soda and mix with the wet ingredients. Fold in the chocolate chips.

4. Roll balls of the dough and place on a baking tray lined with baking parchment. Flatten the balls slightly. Bake for about 12–15 minutes, until golden brown. Leave to cool before serving.

MINI BOILED CLEMENTINE & ALMOND CAKES

These are based on a recipe by Michelle Cranston and these are great for Christmas party season.

PREP TIME: 15 MINS · COOK TIME: 1 HOUR 25 MINS

5 **clementines**

6 **eggs**

150g **coconut sugar**

a few drops of **vanilla extract**

200g **ground almonds**

1 teaspoon **baking powder**

sunflower oil, for greasing

1 **orange**

2 tablespoons **rice malt syrup**

1 teaspoon **poppy seeds**

1. Heat the oven to 180°C/350°F/gas mark 4.

2. Put the clementines into a pan, cover with water and simmer for about 1 hour, making sure the water is topped up and the fruit is always covered. Drain and allow to cool. Blitz the fruit, skin and all, to a purée in a food processor.

3. Whisk the eggs with the sugar and vanilla until pale. Add the puréed fruit. Fold in the ground almonds and baking powder. Divide between 2 greased muffin tins and bake in the oven for 20 minutes.

4. Squeeze the orange and sieve the juice into a small pan. Add the rice malt syrup and boil until thick. Remove the cakes from the tin while still warm and spoon over the orange syrup. Sprinkle with the poppy seeds to serve.

CHRISTMAS PUDDING

Now bring us some figgy pudding, now bring us some figgy pudding, now bring us some figgy pudding, and bring some out here. Jane based this on her sister-in-law Louise's family recipe.

PREP TIME: 15 MINS · SOAK TIME: OVERNIGHT · COOK TIME: 7 HOURS

50g **coconut oil**, melted, plus extra for greasing

75g **gluten-free self-raising flour**

75g **ground almonds**

2 tablespoons **psyllium husks**

½ teaspoon **ground nutmeg**

½ teaspoon **ground cinnamon**

½ teaspoon **mixed spice**

350g **dried mixed fruit**

125g **coconut sugar**

1 large **carrot**, grated

1 **apple**, grated

50g **gluten-free vegetable suet**

1 tablespoon **date syrup**

zest and juice of ½ **orange**

zest of 1 **lemon**

1 **egg**

a good slug of **brandy**

1. Mix all the ingredients together and spoon into a greased pudding bowl. Allow to stand overnight or for 24 hours, adding more alcohol if you like.

2. Cover the pudding bowl with a layer of greaseproof paper and one of foil. Steam for about 4½ hours. Allow to cool, then remove the lid and replace with fresh greaseproof and foil. Leave in a cool place until Christmas.

3. The pudding can be stored in a cool place. To reheat for serving, steam the pudding, as above, for 2½ hours.

APPLE, DATE & ORANGE CRUMBLE

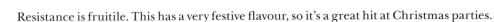

Resistance is fruitile. This has a very festive flavour, so it's a great hit at Christmas parties.

PREP TIME: 20 MINS · COOK TIME: 40 MINS

75g **coconut oil**

150g **gluten-free plain flour**

75g **gluten-free rolled oats**

100g **coconut sugar**

75g **pecans**, chopped

1kg **apples**, peeled and cored

1 large **orange**

12 **dates**, chopped

2 tablespoons **brandy**

1. Heat the oven to 160°C/325°F/gas mark 3.

2. Chop the coconut oil into small pieces and rub into the flour until it resembles breadcrumbs. This can be done in a food processor.

3. Stir in the oats, half the coconut sugar and the pecans and rub all together with your fingertips.

4. Cut the apples into 1–2cm chunks and place in an 25cm ovenproof gratin dish or similar. Zest the orange, then remove the peel and pith from the orange and cut the flesh into 1–2cm pieces. Add the zest and fruit to the apples with the dates, the remaining sugar and the brandy. Mix together.

5. Top the fruit with the crumble mix and bake in the oven for about 40 minutes. Leave to cool slightly before serving.

PEAR & CHOCOLATE CAKE

This is another Queen Bee Cakes recipe. The chocolate and the pear make quite a pair.

PREP TIME: 15 MINS · COOK TIME: 45 MINS

600g **pears** (about 5 large ripe Conference pears), peeled and cut into eighths

200g **coconut sugar**, plus a little extra for the syrup

160g **coconut oil**, melted

3 medium **eggs**, lightly whisked

zest and juice of 1 **orange**

1 teaspoon **vanilla extract**

175g **self-raising gluten-free flour**, sifted

½ teaspoon **baking powder**

125g **sugar-free dark chocolate**, chopped

FOR THE ICING

45g **sugar-free dark chocolate**

15g **coconut butter**

15g **raw honey**

1. Heat the oven to 170°C/350°F/gas mark 3.

2. Mix the pears and 25g of the sugar together in a bowl.

3. Whisk the remaining sugar, coconut oil, eggs, orange zest and vanilla together until light and fluffy. Add the flour, baking powder and chocolate and fold in gently.

4. Place the pear pieces on the bottom layer of a 23cm round, springform cake tin lined with baking parchment, arranging them in a spiral pattern. If you have any pear left over, chop into small pieces and add to the cake mixture.

5. Spoon the cake mixture into the tin on top of the pears, then place in the middle of the oven and bake for 45 minutes, until golden and firm to the touch. Cook for an extra 10–15 minutes if the cake is still soft in the centre. Be careful not to burn the top.

6. While the cake is still warm, turn it out on to a large flat plate (with a sheet of baking parchment paper on it to stop the cake sticking to the plate). Carefully take off the baking parchment from the base of the cake, using a knife if necessary.

7. Warm the orange juice with a little coconut sugar to make a syrup. Drizzle it over the cake, then leave to cool on the plate.

8. Melt the icing ingredients in a bain-marie until silky and smooth. Drizzle the icing over the cake, using a pastry brush (in a criss-cross fashion if you're feeling fancy). Leave to cool before serving.

TREAT YOURSELF

PINEAPPLE, BANANA & COCONUT ICE CREAM

A totally tropical treat.

PREP TIME: 5 MINS · FREEZE TIME: 4 HOURS

½ small **pineapple**, peeled

1 large ripe **banana**

200ml **coconut cream**

1. Dice the flesh of the pineapple into small pieces and slice the banana. Place in a container in the freezer for at least 4 hours.

2. Drain any watery liquid from the coconut cream and place in the freezer. It's also a good idea to freeze a glass bowl to serve the ice cream in.

3. Just before serving, blitz everything together until smooth in a food processor or with a stick blender, pushing down any rough pieces that creep up the side of the bowl. If you're having trouble blending it, you may have to wait for it to melt slightly before whizzing in your powerful processor. Serve in the cold glass bowl immediately.

✓
V
SF

LEON
PALEON BAR

Power up with slow-burning energy that's all hits, no filler. A super hit at our restaurants.

PREP TIME: 10 MINS · COOK TIME: 20 MINS

100g chopped **dates**

100ml **water**

a pinch of **vanilla powder**

2 **eggs**

105g **ground hazelnuts**

105g **ground cashews**

a pinch of **sea salt**

100g **coconut oil**, melted but not hot

50g toasted **pistachios**, roughly chopped

50g **cashews**, roughly chopped

40g **sunflower seeds**

60g **pumpkin seeds**

240g **sugar-free dried cranberries**

1. Heat the oven to 180°C/350°F/gas mark 4.

2. Blend the dates, water and vanilla powder in a high-speed blender until smooth, to make the date paste.

3. Put the date paste into a mixing bowl with the eggs, ground hazelnuts, ground cashews, sea salt and coconut oil. Mix well until combined, then add the chopped nuts, seeds and cranberries.

4. Press the mixture into a 20 x 20cm baking tray lined with greaseproof paper and bake in the oven for 20–22 minutes.

5. Allow to cool in the tray, then cut into squares.

We love the tartness of dried cranberries but, if you prefer, use currants, raisins, or dried strawberries. To make sure these bars are free from refined sugar, read the packet ingredients on your dried fruit to make sure it doesn't contain any added sugar.

RECIPE INDEX

MAIN INDEX

THANK YOU

FROM JANE

First, thank you to the people of Tokelau (it's where David was made) for being a totally Fast and Free nation and my son David for putting up with a few chaotic months • Rachael – because none of this would have happened without her and at least she didn't throw any essential ingredients down the sink • Emin Cheese – for being cheesy and having the best name • Beth – I have a teeny girl crush because she's so fab (and not the precious fashion idiot I thought she was) • Saskia – for managing us all in a kind of steely determined way and for kicking my ass (again) • Jo – the pizza queen and creative design genius • Tom – for stealing my thunder with the Kofte recipe (and pouncing around being photographed for far too long and loving it) • Tamin – great pics and lovely to work with, although I feel his future is in Page 3 • Steph – a diamond in every respect and a calming influence on us all • Lara and Martin for hosting us at Coombe Farm Studios in Dittisham • Beth and Liam for being fab assistants and choppers extrodinaire • Louise Haines at Fourth Estate for her kind permission to reprint the Asian Prawn Pancakes recipe • Octopus lot !

FROM JOHN

Until books write themselves (hopefully a long time after cars drive themselves) it takes a lot of people to make a LEON book happen. Jane and I have been so grateful for the love and graft of two people in particular: Saskia and Jo. This love and graft is the basis of an amazing partnership: Saskia is the overall boss and the boss of logistics, editing and joy, while Jo is the boss of design and art work. Between them they have helped Jane and me make sure the book you have in your hand is our 'best' work.

The photography is all down to Tamin Jones whose skill is matched by his character. When you are spending long and yet intense hours with a photographer it makes such a difference when they are positive, can-do and can bend themselves into lots of different positions (including lying on the ground) in order to show the food in its best light. Thank you Tamin. And thank you too to Tamin's assistant Steph who made the photos possible, as well as often making the party.

One of those party places was the comely Coombe Farm in Devon where Lara and her husband Martin hosted us all. I think she enjoyed the upside of eating with us, but went well beyond the norm in showing hospitality. Including letting me join the all-female yoga class in my Lycra shorts.

Beth Morgan and Liam Chau were fantastic food assistants.

Thank you too to Millie Hempleman and Tara Hesseltine, who made sure we were all 'propped up'.

I owe so much too to Wendy Mandy who is a wise, beautiful friend and guide.

Thank you to my many advisers and to people who have backed Leon with their time and counsel: Jane Melvin, Nick Evans, Tim Smalley, Spencer Skinner, Jacques Fragis, Brad Blum, Jimmy Allen, Steve Head, Scott Uehlein, Bob Mock, Mike Ellis, Vivian Imerman and Gavyn Davies.

Meleni Aldridge from Bite the Sun has advised us for the last two years on nutrition, and also wrote the science bits in this book. And Angela Dowden checked all of the nutritional icons, quite a few times.

Carole Symons has, from the beginning of Leon, used all of her scientific and persuasive skills to decry gluten and dairy and sugar.

The shoots needed extra LEON hands and Rachael, Beth and Emin provided them with vigour.

Our publishing team (or 'punk sighing' team as my autocorrect just wrote) is a heavenly group of people led by Alison Starling (who can also be nicely strict) and Jonathan Christie from the creative direction side and Pauline Bache the editor. Thanks too to the PR and marketing teams who have hopefully by now stopped this book from being a secret.

Antony Topping our literary agent has been important to making this happen and has sprayed on the odd WD40 where the process needed it.

All we do now and in the future started in Carnaby Street in 2004 where Henry and Allegra and I began this adventure. Thank you both of you for your support and for all the DNA you (hygienically) injected into LEON. Thank you everyone who works at Leon today and who has been in the gang since 2004.

Thank you Katie for being the most supportive wife a hyperactive man could have and to my fantastic daughters Natasha and Eleanor for your love. My Mum Marion is the most positive person I know and inspires all I do. Well, most of what I do. And of course to my Dad LEON who inspired us a little with our name.

THE LEON FAMILY

Abdelhadi Fekier
Abdullah Mamun
Aboubacar Sanoko
Abril Marcozzi Ahumada
Adam Hon Adam Blaker
Adam Jaworski
Adam Klosowski
Adam Nagy
Ademola Akande
Adetayo John Toye
Adrian Fernandez Jodar
Adrian Pompey
Adriano Paduano
Agnes Hochheiser
Ahmed Ahamada
Ahmed Hussain
Akli Ouarab
Alaina Cisotto
Alan McNiven
Alastair Delaney
Alberto Biasi
Alejandra Martinez
Aleksandra Maj
Alessandro Perleonardi
Alessandro Straccia
Alessia Caberlon
Alessio Marcon
Alex Horwood
Alexander Jean-Baptiste
Alexandra Bacsi
Alexandra Haya
Alexandra Hrinova
Alexandra Liedtke
Alexandrei Lambon
Alexandru Campean
Alexandru Cotici
Alfred Russo
Algirdas Visockis
Alina Leonte
Alisson Grossi
Aljaz Rozenicnik
Allegra Bulferi
Althea Grittini
Alvaro Martin
Amal Noureddine
Amandine Hastoy
Amaury Brusacoram
Amir Astab Hussain
Ana Gututui
Ana Lisman
Ana Minguez
Ana Nobrega Quijano
Ana Pereira Nobrega
Ana Sobrinho

Ana Rita Coelho De Castro
Anabel Guerrero
Anastasija Krickovska
Anderson Gomcalves
Andoni Ibanez Garcia
Andras Klug
Andrea Bassi
Andrea Bulgarelli
Andrea Caratozzolo
Andrea Franchi
Andrea Gil Coll
Andrea Pisci
Andrei Barcau
Andreia Ivascu
Andres Parra Gracia
Angela Antonou
Angelica Vallone
Anna Kormos
Anna Kruk
Anna Llevadias
Anna Swietlicka
Anna Julia Forsell
Palmcrantz
Anna Maria Gioia Ramillano
Antal Babarczi
Anthony Anyetei
Anthony Pierre
Antoinette Xaviera
Antonella Primavera
Antonia Forsythe
Antony Perring
Anwar Sebbah El-Kachachi
Arianna Rosone
Aridane Hernadez
Armani Leroy
Arthur Toso
Arti Dhrona
Asher Spencer
Ashraf Khalifa Mahgoub
Asia Dantoni
Aurelie Diz
Bairish Pushpakanthan
Bartlomiej Chlebanowski
Beatrice Gessa
Ben Iredale
Bence Kovacs
Bernardo Aragao
Bernardo Delgado
Hernandez
Berta Kargaudaite
Bertrand Rameaux
Beth Emmens
Bettina Szabo
Beverley Morgan

Bibiana Adamova
Blanca Lossio Diaz
Blendina Islami
Bola Adako
Borbala Simon
Bouchaib Bouida
Bree Faucher
Brittany Henderson
Bruna Lise De Moura
Caina Bertussi Rotta
Callum Cound
Cameron Essam
Carla Louro
Carlo Poli
Carlos Izquierdo
Carmen Villanueva Garcia
Carolyn Prieur
Cedric Hoffman
Cengiz Rahmioglu
Cesar Alvarez Gallego
Cesar Fernandez
Chad Hyndman
Chanta Octave
Charlene Haughton
Charlene Le Brigand
Charlotte McCarter
Chevonne Robinson
Chiara Donadoni
Chineye Nnamani
Christian Camilli
Christopher Burford
Chuphangini
Chandrakanthan
Cinzia Bastianello
Cinzia Oliviero
Claire Didier
Claire Ollivier
Clara Ballesteros
Clara Bleda Megias
Claudia Costea
Claudia Lagana
Claudinei Da Silva
Cleiton Francisco Da Silva
Clement Claeys
Comfort Babirye
Concetta Arduino
Connor Diver
Cora Forsdick
Corey Douglas
Courtnee Cropp
Craig Wright
Cristina Tonucci
Cristina Tudor
Csaba Borsos

Csaba Lukacs
Daniel Gomez Gomez
Daniela Campos Cruz
Daniela-Claudia Varvarei
Daveline Lionel
David Biro
David Del Rio
David Gera
David O'Leary
Davide Omizzolo
Debbie Thorpe
Debra Maccow
Deepak Lalaji
Denis Rivers Coakley
Desire Bonilla
Desiree Ortiz Saameno
Devni Liyanage
Diane Bolumbo
Dimitar Dimitrov
Djillali Djellal
Dmitrijs Cumacenko
Dmitrijs Iljins
Dominik Bodo
Dora Bleaga
Dovydas Bronusas
Edit Marton
Edson Cadete
Edvinas Marma
El Mehdi Chaouqi
Elin Thomas
Elisa Medd Canete
Elisa Piazza
Elisa Poli
Elisa Pompa
Elizabeth Nobrega Quijano
Elizabeth Olaleye
Elizabeth Oloyede
Elizangela Ravaneda
Elsayed Mohamed
Emanuele Giordano
Emilios Patounas
Emily Hawkley
Emily-Ann Cheese
Emmanuel Saliu
Engila Saidy
Eniolywa Adeyemi
Enrica Latorre
Enrico Bonetti
Erika Fernandez Priegue
Erika Garcia
Erika Gatti
Erika Kupfer
Erika Perna
Erzsebet Hobora

Estibaliz Pena Barbara
Eva Zacharia
Ewan Milne
Ewelina McDonald
Fabio Paixao Da Conceicao Santos
Fabio Prandi
Fabio Rodrigues
Fabio Rosa
Fabio Soliman
Fatma Abdurahman
Federica Masciulli
Federico Bazan
Federico Cau
Felice Catania
Felipe Mesa Koch
Fernando Blanco Gutierrez De Rueda
Filippo Ciarla
Flora Pap
Fontana Clemente
Frances Moran
Francesca Balia
Francesco Basile
Francesco Festevole
Francisco Jimenez San Nicolas
Frederique Anctil
Gabor Salai
Gabriella Kovacs
Gallad Musa
Gary Marriott
Gary Scarboro
Gema Madueno Lada
Gemma Kearney
Georgios Kogkos
Gerard Ribalta I Vivas
Giacomo Medda
Giada Rosignoli
Gianluca Marletta
Gianmarco Abramo
Giorgia Orfei
Giorgia Scaramagli
Giorgio Mancino
Giovanna Fuentes
Giovanna Gargiulo
Giulia Chiominto
Giulia Palmarini
Giuseppe Crielesi
Giuseppe Laporta
Giuseppe Marsiglia
Giuseppi Bargione
Glenn Edwards
Gonzalo Perpina Llorca
Graham Brown
Guido Modena
Gustavo Batistella
Gyongy Matyas
Hafdala Buyema

Hamza Harrat
Hana Abdullah
Hana Pavlovicova
Handan Argun
Hannah Adamson
Hannah Redfearn
Hannah Thomas
Hector Fernandez
Hector Morillo Aguilera
Holly Clare
Hsiang Liao
Ignacio Curtolo
Ilaria De Tommaso
Ina Chiperi
Ines Sineiro
Ines Maria Da Costa De Sepulveda
Ioannis Chaniotakis
Irene Magula
Isabella Noce
Istvan Szep
Iuliana Gaita
Izabela Kaniuk
Jada Kennedy-Mark
Jade Ebejer
Jakub Jacek Adamczewski
James Adewale
Jamie Watts
Jane Eagles
Javier Medina Selles
Javier Santos
Jelena Cumacenko
Jemel Roache
Jenny Di Nunzio
Jesse Jaiquel Martin
Jessica Dolu
Jessica Gonzalez Rios
Jessica Johnstone
Jesus Antonio Tabares Zuniga
Jhun Alkonga
Jimena Del Rosario Cenzano Vicuna
Jiri Czolko
Joanna Buczowska
Joanne Letremy
Jo Ormiston
Joao Freitas
Joao Ribeiro Da Silva
Joao Venda
Joel Brogan
Joelle Bisimwa
Joelle Davis
John Brooks
John Corrigan
John Scott
John Upton
John Vincent
Jorge Palomo Campos

Jorge Valls Laguarda
Jose Maria Arez De Vilhena Alves Rafael
Josep Oriol Ortega Matas
Joshua Prynn-Petit
Judit Alonso Rodriguez
Julio Velezmoro
Justin Ovenden
Justyna Strozyk
Kamila Kilian
Kamran Foladi
Karolina Blazewicz
Kashmira John
Katalin Egyed
Katalin Szabo
Katarzyna Jur
Katia Mendes
Katie Jones
Katya Yovcheva
Kayanda Besa
Kayleigh Goodger
Kelly Coakley
Kelly Lenis Garcia
Kendra Guerrero Marin
Kimberly Ferenc-Batchelor
Kinga Sarvary
Kiril Guglya
Kirsty Adamson
Kirsty Saddler
Kofi Yeboah - Fordjour
Konstantinos Kyziridis
Kristen Rego
Kristina Dabkeviciene
Kristina Kocenaite
Lakshmi Pillay
Larissa Simpson-Brown
Latifah Stone
Laura Espana Saez
Laura Esteban
Laura Stoppini
Layla Mcdougall
Leah Johnson-Nesbitt
Lee Dunning
Lidia Budkowska
Liliya Georgieva
Linda Fischerova
Livio Pierro
Liviu Haulica
Lob Tang
Loredana Tota
Loui-James Lauder
Luca Bargione
Luca Berardi
Luca Galvanelli
Luca La Terra
Luca Lamera
Luca Scazzola
Lucie Schubertova
Lucja Szyszka

Lucrezia Corradi
Lucy Humphrey
Luigi Longobardi
Lukasz Kubiak
Lukasz Ludowich
Lydia Tuker
Lynda Elbounabi
Maciej Kosecki
Maciej Meyza
Maciej Urbanski
Macijauskas Ignas
Magdalena Sierocka
Mahomed Azouz
Maksim Belov
Malgorzata Herda
Malgorzata Pasierb
Manon Joly
Manrique Sancho Caraballeda
Manuel Alvarez Leon
Manuela Crivellari
Marcia Preciosa
Marcin Kaminski
Marco Berardi
Marco Pistilli
Marco Spada
Marcos Diaz-Delgado
Margarita Cadavid Moreno
Maria Belenguer Manzanedo
Maria Cabello Muriana
Maria D'Addio
Maria De Las Heras Bravo
Maria Ghezzi
Maria Reales Garcia
Maria Clara Iudica
Maria Eduarda Moreira
Mariana Kastrati
MariaRosaria Falanga
Marisha David
Marta Konik
Marta Matulewicz
Marta Sedano Vera
Marta Velasco Leonor
Martin Sanchez
Martina Ciccora
Martina Radochova
Martyn Trigg
Mateusz Koziolek
Matteo Di Cugno
Matteo Losito
Matteo Riccobene
Matteo Roscini
Matthew Ali
Matthew Hayden-Baker
Matthew Oakes
Matthew Slaunwhite
Maurizio Ciaburra
Mauro Curtolo

Maxime Roseau
Meenakshi Guirous
Melissa Wilson
Melitta Bicsar
Mercedes Martin
Meymouna Guaye
Michaela Stokoe
Michaela Winter
Michal Urlewicz
Micheline Essomba
Miguel Munoz
Mihaela Sassu
Mihaela Zhivkova
Mirko Antonucci
Mohammed Asmul
Mohammedanwar Sumro
Monica Cardoso
Monika Jagla
Monika Kwiatkowska
Moses Abimbola
Mourad Meghlaoui
Nadea Ahmed
Nadeige Tshiala
Nadiuska De Lourdes
Spranger Santos
Naiara Rodenas Capote
Nainasara Thada Magar
Natalia Kosicka
Natalia Suarez Jimenez
Natalie Birikorang
Natalie Liow
Nataliya Dimitrova
Natasha Cowdrey
Nathan Lewis
Nenko Stoyadinov
Nestor Fernandez
Nhung Le
Nichola Norton
Nicholas Scovell
Nicola Settecase
Nicolas Kupfer Subi
Nikola Vrtiskova
Nikoletta Berta
Nina Amaniampong
Nina Jaworska
Nina Jullien
Niravkumar Desai
Nomsa Mangena
Nora Polacsek
Nundi Parsons
Nunzio Panico
Nuwan Polambe Gedara
Oja Simon
Oktawiusz Kawecki
Olegs Nikolajevs
Olga Chodorowska
Olga Murszakajeva
Oluwatobiloba Olutayo
On Yee Annie Lo

Ona Curto Graupera
Orla Delargy
Orsolya Lazar-Erdelyi
Oskar Zawodniak
Otoa Ise
Ozgur Kuden
Pablo Garcia
Pablo Olalla Vilches
Pascual Micha Avomo
Patricia Rodriguez
Patrick McKenny
Paul Casey
Paul Farmer
Paulo Rodrigues
Pawel Szyszka
Pedro Barchin Perez
Peter Bakai
Peter Meszaros
Petya Zhivkova
Philip Salousti
Philippa Dando
Rabbani Mahbuby
Rabbil Dewan
Rabson Mwale
Rachael Gough
Rachel Austin
Radoslaw Zemsta
Rafael Mendes
Rafal Nowak
Raimundas Melkunas
Raj Halder
Ramona Alexandrescu
Raquel Pascual
Rasa Raskeviciute
Rebeca Calugareanu
Rebecca Di Mambro
Rebecca Kallaghe
Reda el Guebli
Remigijus Chmieliauskas
Remy Le Mentec
Renatas Kacinskas
Rexford Odai
Rhea Peacock
Rianna Alexander-Harris
Ricardo Blanco Sanchez
Ricardo Braun
Ritika Nowlakha
Roberta Adamo
Roberta Bosco
Roberta Rimkute
Roberto Curati
Robinson Garzon
Rodrigo Moreno Fuentes
Romain Brun
Romain Chaillol
Roozbeh Emadmodaresi
Rui Mesquita
Russell Simpson
Rute Valente Coelho Da

Rocha Barreiros
Ruth Chanter
Ruth Johnson-Nesbitt
Ruth Saliu
Sabrina Stefan
Saffron Cann
Salvatore Polizzi
Salvija Dargyte
Sam Kenney-herbert
Samara Addai
Samir Goumrar
Samuel McIntyre
Samuel Rance
Sandra Barriuso
Sandra Navarro
Sara Sanchez Rodrigo
Sarra Tesheme
Saskia Sidey
Sebastian Lapiedra Franco
Sephora Martinez
Serena Bersani
Serena Cecchinato
Serena Micciche
Sergi Cerezo I Martinez
Sergio Garcia Alfaro
Sergio Paniego Blanco
Sergiu Chirilenco
Servet Ozturk
Severina Pascale
Shanti Pun
Sheela Thapa
Shereene Garrison
Shewit Weldegiorgis
Shirine Shah
Shyanne Watson
Sienam Akotey
Silvia Masala
Silvia Zuccarino
Simona Donato
Simona Pugliese
Simona Sodringa
Simone Abbate
Simone Florian
Simone Messina
Simone Pittiglio
Sophie Kaye
Soufian Khatib
Stacey Little
Stacey Strachan
Stefania Paratore
Stefano Pinto
Stephanie Agyemang
Stephen Oliver
Stiven Fernandez
Mondragon
Suada Fetahu
Suna Lee
Szabolcs Szasz
Tadas Tamilinas

Taehoon Jeong
Tamara Hernandez
Tamas Babarczi
Tammy-lee Goodger
Tanya Parratt
Thabiso Moyo
Thiago Turibio Da Silva
Thomas Davies
Thomas Green
Thomas Malley
Thomas Villa
Tierney Faucher
Tom Shephard
Tomas Canet Estornell
Tommaso Marano
Tommaso Venegoni
Tonya Moralez
Tsvetelina Lazarova
Tunde Vig
Ullahelena Wane Ndembo
Vaiva Gaudutyte
Valentin Dragan
Valentino Esposito
Valeria Angelova
Valeria Colesanti
Vanessa Dos Santos
Vanessza Kobli
Vasilica Cirican
Vendella Bubu-
Oppenheimer
Vendula Kozova
Veronica Scotto Di Perta
Victoria Kuziora
Vieri Martini
Viktor Kanasz
Viktorija Kapustina
Vito Rubino
Viviane Bogdanov Simao
Vivien Walker
Vuyolwethu Vundla
Wanda Perretta
William Caddick
Wojciech Antoniewicz
Yasmin Mesquita
Yasmine Rajim
Yemima Walet Ibrahim
Yenny Chong
Ylenia Bermudez Sanchez
Zahidul Islam
Zara Mughal
Zaynab Ali
Zilvinas Gryte
Zoe Cuartas
Zoe Grant
Zoe Masson-Herve
Zsofia Szabo
Zsuzsanna Szalkai
Zunezo Sadiq
Zydrune Petrauskaite

THE LEON FAMILY

An Hachette UK Company
www.hachette.co.uk

First published in Great Britain in 2017 by Conran Octopus,
a division of Octopus Publishing Group Ltd
Carmelite House, 50 Victoria Embankment
London EC4Y 0DZ
www.octopusbooks.co.uk

ISBN 978-1-84091-710-9

A CIP catalogue record for this book is available
from the British Library.

Printed and bound in Italy

10 9 8 7 6 5 4 3 2

PHOTOGRAPHY BY TAMIN JONES

Publisher: Alison Starling
Senior editor: Pauline Bache
Art direction, styling and design (for LEON): Jo Ormiston
Creative director: Jonathan Christie
Copywriter and brand manager (for LEON): Saskia Sidey
Recipe nutritional analysis: Angela Dowden
Additional 'Why Free-from' text: Meleni Aldridge
Photography assistant: Stephanie Howard
Copyeditor: Annie Lee
Senior production manager: Katherine Hockley

We have endeavoured to be as accurate as possible in all the
preparation and cooking times listed in the recipes in this
book. However they are an estimate based on our own timings
during recipe testing, and should be taken as a guide only, not
as the literal truth. Nutrition advice is not absolute. If you feel
you require consultation with a nutritionist, consult your GP
for a recommendation.

Standard level spoon measurements are used in all recipes.
1 tablespoon = one 15 ml spoon
1 teaspoon = one 5 ml spoon

Eggs should be medium unless otherwise stated. The
Department of Health advises that eggs should not be
consumed raw. This book contains dishes made with raw or
lightly cooked eggs. It is prudent for more vulnerable people
such as pregnant and nursing mothers, invalids, the elderly,
babies and young children to avoid uncooked or lightly cooked
dishes made with eggs. Once prepared these dishes should be
kept refrigerated and used promptly.

Fresh herbs should be used unless otherwise stated. If
unavailable use dried herbs as an alternative but halve the
quantities stated.

Ovens should be preheated to the specific temperature – if
using a fan-assisted oven, follow manufacturer's instructions
for adjusting the time and the temperature.

This book includes dishes made with nuts and nut derivatives.
It is advisable for customers with known allergic reactions to
nuts and nut derivatives and those who may be potentially
vulnerable to these allergies, such as pregnant and nursing
mothers, invalids, the elderly, babies and children, to avoid
dishes made with nuts and nut oils. It is also prudent to
check the labels of pre-prepared ingredients for the possible
inclusion of nut derivatives.

Vegetarians should look for the 'V' symbol on a cheese to
ensure it is made with vegetarian rennet. There are vegetarian
forms of Parmesan, Feta, Cheddar, Cheshire, Red Leicester,
dolcelatte and many goats' cheeses, among others.

Not all soy sauce is gluten-free – we use tamari (a gluten-free
type of soy sauce), but check the label if you are unsure.

Remember to check the labels on ingredients to make sure
they don't have hidden refined sugars. Even savoury goods
can be artificially sweetened so it's always best to check the
label carefully.

ABOUT THE AUTHORS
JANE BAXTER

Jane Baxter is the co-author of *Leon Happy Salads* with John
Vincent and *Leon Fast Vegetarian* with Henry Dimbleby. She
also co-authored *The Riverford Farm Cook Book*, which won Best
First Book at the Guild of Food Writers' Awards. Jane worked
at the Carved Angel in Dartmouth and the River Cafe London
before becoming the Head Chef at the Field Kitchen, the
restaurant for Riverford Organic Vegetables. She now spends
her time catering, consulting on food matters and hosting
food events in unusual locations.

JOHN VINCENT

John Vincent is the Co-founder of Leon, which now has more
than 45 restaurants across the UK. He wrote the bestselling
Leon Naturally Fast Food with Henry Dimbleby, *Leon Family &
Friends* with Kay Plunkett-Hogge and *Leon Happy Salads* with
Jane Baxter. John co-wrote the Government's School Food
Plan, with Leon co-founder Henry Dimbleby, which resulted in
practical cooking and nutrition being put on the curriculum
for the first time, and free school lunches for all infant
children. John likes food, and Jane.